TRAITMATCH

Discovering the Occupational Personality Through Handwriting Analysis

by

Eldene Whiting

International Resources   Pismo Beach CA

1989

©1989 by Eldene Whiting

First Printing 1977
Second Printing 1982
Third Printing 1985
Fourth Printing (Second Edition) 1989

LC: 77-837-29
ISBN: 0-937480-02-9

Printed in the United States of America

Published by International Resources
          A Division of Padre Productions
          P.O. Box 3113
          Pismo Beach, California 93449

The author and the publishers acknowledge the contribution of Peter Blazi, co-author of the first edition of Traitmatch *which appeared under the imprint of Vulcan Books of Seattle.*

TRAITMATCH fits the right person to the right job in a simple, unusual and effective way!

A book for employers, counselors, personnel managers—anyone who hires—and for the job-seeker as well.

What do businessmen say who have used handwriting analysis?

"I am completely convinced of its usefullness."

"...extremely pleased with the results...an immensely valuable tool."

"In all the testing I have used in the past twenty years, I haven't found any as thorough as the handwriting analysis."

"I have depended on it as a daily guide...in the business and professional world."

Eldene Whiting
Certified Graphologist

Also by the Author:
Holistic Graphology
Printing, The Graphologist's Enigma
Writing the Analysis
Doodles Diagnosed

Table of Contents

Introduction to the Second Edition

Traitmatch is a specialized work, representing a narrow but extremely useful aspect of the wide range of material included in handwriting analysis as a field of study. There are many general descriptive books to be found listed in the Selected References. The goal of *Traitmatch* is to offer a clear and practical application of graphological principles to those who work in business and in the helping services, such as law, medicine, psychology, crime investigation, sociology and related areas. It is used by specialists in personnel selection, family and marriage counseling, school and college advisement, career education, and vocational counseling.

From the outset, *Traitmatch* was intended to serve as a practical handbook for professionals. Reprinted with slight revision six years after its first publication, it gained acceptance as a text by some graphology teachers. Business people used it for reference. In recent years it has reached an expanded audience, with orders from professionals in Europe. At the same time, the technological changes of our computer world have made a thorough revision necessary. Old job descriptions have vanished and new ones have emerged. Emphasis is on service and technical jobs, managerial skills and meeting foreign competition for worldwide markets.

The initial reason for writing *Traitmatch* is still intact. It is still a primer for the uninitiated in the art/science of graphology. It is still a valuable tool for selecting personnel and avoiding hiring prejudice. It is still an excellent method for shifting employees to the assignment that is most positive and satisfying.

With this new edition the reader should find even more practical use for graphology in the daily business environment. We have expanded the job descriptions, the vocational requirements, and the analyses to help you find current applications in handwriting examples.

Traitmatch is intended to meet the needs of prospective employees, employers and personnel managers, and teachers of graphology. The focus is on the use of graphology in the everyday business world.

Seldom does a prospective employee consider his or her special personal needs and match their native talents with potential job skills. Get the job—then try to fit the personality into job requirements—is the usual sequence of action. No wonder 80 per cent of the working public is unhappy in their jobs! Until recently once the job was secure it was heresy to consider greener grass elsewhere. But in this age of rapid and continuous change we no longer demand that a man or woman remain static in one job for the thirty plus years that constitute a career. Why does it take an economic, health or marital earthquake to dislodge a person from a job he or she hates? Why not plan the change intelligently?

All change is painful. It takes courage to make the decision to change jobs. But if the choice is yours alone *Traitmatch* can help you to understand yourself better and make a career change with greater comfort and intelligence. A thorough analysis of your handwriting is the first step. This should be done by a professional analyst who has been consulting in personnel selection for some years. Such an analysis can be the open sesame to an exciting new adventure. Try it. You'll be surprised.

For the employer *Traitmatch* saves time, money and headaches. As long as we have human beings we will have time wasters, square pegs, addictive personalities, liars and cheats. Employers interview prospective employees to eliminate these headaches. The employee interview is the essential pre-hire tool. Employee handbooks, goverment bulletins, seminars and books all warn that today's interviews are filled with legal pitfalls. There are scores of questions the employer can't ask. But there's no law against considering a handwritten application or sample.

Besides intellect, leadership qualities and compatibility, *Traitmatch* is an excellent evaluator for the negative traits of poor health, alcohol or drug addiction, disloyalty and dishonesty. Employers don't need these headaches. There's no point in hiring these negatives, spending time and money training the employee to your methods, then having to fire one for incompetence later. Avoid these headaches in the first place by screening out potential trouble.

In over a decade of use, *Traitmatch* has been of repeated help to employees and employers. Industry has turned increasingly to using handwriting analysis in personnel selection. The professional graphologists have helped to bring about this acceptance of the techniques through improving the standards of practioners.

Consolidation of several national professional groups under the umbrella of a Council of Graphological Societies has helped to bring together experienced analysts who develop new standards and techniques of excellence through academic research and stronger ethics.

Although *Traitmatch* is not designed to be used primarily as a text book, many teachers often refer to its simple methods and examples. The book has become a product, not just of two minds, but of many who have helped mold and refine the contents into the present product. Jean Calori C.G. of Graphology Consultants and Charlie Cole C.G., who founded the American Handwriting Analysis Foundation, gave unstinting of materials and expertise. I thank those who helped guide the business data; Milton Tichlin, Ph.D., Dr. Jordan Detzler, Gene Lepre, Randy Mason and Bill Robinson of the San Diego Police Department. I also want to thank those many people who provided writing samples including Dave Oliver, Paula Sassi C.G., Gayle Price, Robert Gale, and Beverly Barich.

It was Peter Blazi who first approached me about writing a book on personnel selection using handwriting analysis. For two years we struggled with the concepts, format and approach to the subject. I appreciated his initial contribution greatly and regret he was not available to assist in the second edition.

In addition the patience of Arlene Richardson during the original effort and of Bob Whiting during the subsequent reprints have given me support that cannot be measured. Lachlan P. MacDonald and Karen L. Reinecke have added the expertise and suggestions to create the improved and expanded book that *Traitmatch* is. Bless you all.

Eldene Whiting

"A non-perfectable science would not be a science, and our numerous disciples one day will make it work after us by developments the inventor himself did not suspect when he laid down the first basics."

Jean-Hyppolite Michon
Founder of Graphology

CHAPTER 1

The Successful Secret Business Won't Share

Recently a major insurance firm doubled the number of its "million-dollar salesmen," valuable men who had sold more than one million dollars in life insurance coverage. The reason? The agency was now using handwriting analysis to select its employees.

A company that furnished and decorated model homes reduced its employee turnover rate from thirty percent to *zero* in one year and increased sales over 170%! The sales manager had learned the advantages of using the science of graphology (handwriting analysis) to evaluate applicants before hiring them.

The most useful tool for choosing the right person for the right job is by discovering the *occupational personality* through handwriting analysis. No other method of character evaluation can expose so much about an individual in so little time and with such accuracy. Yet many companies hesitate to use it. Those that do are reluctant to admit it. Some even deny it.

Why? Most likely, businesses that use graphology appreciate the additional leverage against competition. Also, the uncanny revelations gleaned from the written word originally linked graphology to the supernatural. Its accuracy so amazed the general public that dime-store mystics and carnival operators were quicker to see its financial rewards than was industry. The memory lingers on, like a respected schoolteacher with a shady past.

Today, graphology is over a century old and recognized as a science by most of the civilized world. European companies like

Lloyds of London use it routinely. In the United States, handwriting analysis is a valuable though private tool helping psychologists, personnel directors, managers, teachers and medical doctors to find answers never thought possible before.

The Hiring Hassle

The dilemma of hiring the right person has become an awesome and complex responsibility. Concerned with mounting turnover rates and unsatisified employees, industrial psychologists continue to research and evaluate the two most commonly used methods of job selection—testing and interviewing. The more these traditional selection techniques are studied, the more appalling the findings.

Bias In Testing

There are as many types of preemployment tests today as there are nervous people taking them: achievement tests, aptitude tests, sensorimotor tests, muscular and perceptual tests. Also there are tests for intelligence, personality and general knowledge.

Professional testers boast of tests which can screen out unsatisfactory employees. In other words, if you are a personnel director, you can now give a test that will show you who you don't want *after* you've already hired them!

Is all of this testing worth the considerable expense in time and money? Researchers are pessimistic. In "Psychology in Industrial Organizations" Norman Maier states that tests for placement "frequently do not sample relevant abilities and thus have low validity." Often people who pass tests turn out to be square pegs, people who fail sometimes make excellent employees.

Bias in testing has been giving industry headaches for a long time. Some relief came from the Civil Rights Act of 1964 restricting tests to those which are "not designed, intended or used to discriminate because of race, color, sex, or national origin." The Equal Opportunity Act of 1972 and other hiring laws have provided the Equal Employment Opportunity Commission the tools necessary to enforce test validation if it appears employers are using tests to discriminate in their hiring practices. Later, we will discuss how the use of Traitmatch can help eliminate these hiring predjudices.

12

Testing shouldn't be entirely neglected in the selection process. The ability to type, read notes of music, repair a transmission or any other specific mechanical skill can best be determined by a performance test for the skill sought. Society, however, has come a long way since workers were considered to be just machines to increase productivity. The higher needs of self-worth and personal fulfillment still elude even the most extensive batteries of tests. In Traitmatch, these values are highly regarded and evaluated as part of the occupational personality.

The Deception Game: The Job Interview

Has this happened to you at least once or twice in your lifetime?

You're sitting across the desk from the personnel director of the company where you want to go to work. He's a pleasant fellow, even if some of his questions do seem rather embarrassing. You smile anyway, trying to make the best impression you can. You answer to please him, even if it doesn't reflect how you really feel.

You mentally total up your goofs, weighing them against your overall effect on the interview—dazzling, disappointing, or downright devastating?

While you're wondering if your antiperspirant will last long enough to get you through this ordeal, research has shown that the personnel director already made his decision within the first four minutes of the interview. His final judgment wasn't based on your qualifications or even on the needs of the company. He decided to hire or reject you by how near your thinking and feeling came to his!

Professional interviewers are also victims of this unreliable tradition. They recognize their own bias to be present and attempt to be as objective and fair as possible when evaluating applicants. Unfortunately, research has also shown that these well-meaning interviewers, while admitting the interview is as useless as gossip, unknowingly gave it great weight in their final hiring decision.

If you later received word that you were selected for the job, your glow of success might have been tarnished by the uneasy anticipation of trying to live up to that unreal image of yourself that you had displayed at the interview.

If you didn't get the job, you probably felt the interview was one of the reasons because it wasn't the "real me" that was rejected—and you'd be absolutely right!

In the traditional mechanics of the job interview, deception is the name of the game—from both sides of the desk.

A wonderful advantage of the use of handwriting analysis over job interviewing is that the job-seeker doesn't have to be present, eliminating tension and embarrassment. Consider the results that are possible to achieve with Traitmatch, where all of this play-acting and critical game-playing simply doesn't exist.

The Secret Exposed

While some companies continue to pour money down the drain supporting the antiquated selection system of testing and interviewing, some others, in desperation, have shifted emphasis toward employee satisfaction and retention *after* the hiring has been done. But that's like thumbing frantically through the pages of a book on how to swim as your doomed vessel slips quickly into the waves—you may survive, and you may not.

Obviously the best solution is to find the right person for the job from the very beginning, *before* hiring. This is when the written words of the applicant in the hands of a person skilled in Traitmatch become worth their weight in company gold.

Applying the same techniques as the professional graphologist—combining and evaluating signs in writing—you will be able to achieve reliable, even extraordinary results.

"Companies generally aren't going to stick out their necks and admit that they use handwriting analysis until more people consider it valid and completely acceptable," says Renee C. Martin, president of Handwriting Consultants, Inc., New York. But here are some comments by businesspeople who have employed graphology successfully in their business, people who have the courage to risk the derision of others while laughing all the way to the bank—people who help expose the secret that business won't share:

"If a man doesn't show up well on the handwriting, we're liable to turn him down."

Robert W. Buckenberg, Vice-president, Sales
Guaranty Reserve Life Insurance Company
Hammond, Indiana
(Wall Street Journal, June 20, 1974)

"I can't emphasize too much that handwriting analysis as an assessment device for hiring personnel does work...it will save you money; it will save you time; it will save you headaches."

Karey Starmer
General Manager
Color Service
San Jose, California
(Courtesy Charles Cole)

"When we ignore the handwriting reports and hire on personal impressions, we make some bad mistakes." Note: This company experienced a 40% decrease in turnover rates.

Ralph Steil
Manager
Prudential Life Insurance Company
San Francisco, California
(The Office, December 1970)

"My experience with people we have hired from whom handwriting analyses were secured prior to their employment substantiate the accuracy of the graphology analysis, and I must say after two years of experience with the technique I have become completely convinced of its usefullness."

John M. Biggs
President
Trend Graphics
Mountain View, California
(Courtesy Charles Cole)

"...graphoanalysis can tell a lot about a man that neither the pre-employment interview nor an objective test can reveal...the final decision in personnel selection rests, of course, with the manager's or general agent's hiring practice. But who would not use the most valuable help he can get in hiring good people?"

Thomas Fullmer
Manager
Standard Insurance Company
Arizona Agency
(Best's Review-Life Edition, June 1971)

How It Works

It's likely you've used handwriting analysis to some degree already. For instance, after your lunch break, you discover a note on your desk. It might be from your secretary, your business partner or your lover. It mght be from your secretary who is also your business partner *and* lover! Who knows?

You do! You've analyzed the note to determine who it's from. It's impossible to remain unmoved by that note or *any* piece of writing, no matter who it's from or what the circumstances.

The graphology that most of us use every day is limited to the recognition of the writing and the reader's interpretation of the writer's thoughts, as expressed in his written words. But writing can tell you more than that. Much more!

Your first hint that handwriting analysis is capable of revealing personality traits may have come from a casual acquaintance who had studied graphology. He'd pick out a certain type of *t*-bar, *i*-dot or lower loop and exclaim, "A-ha! This means so-and-so!" This is known as trait-stroke analysis and it's the kind of graphology that is quite popular across the cocktail table or at social gatherings—and it works! It can be rather frightening to have a stranger tell you things about yourself you thought were well hidden.

An experienced handwriting analyst can read personality traits immediately while a friend must know you for some time before he discovers the same things about you. There's no magic about it. You are made up of the same characteristics that most other people have, but you will emphasize some of them more than others. You use them for motivations in your daily living. It's just common sense that your thought patterns will show up in your handwriting.

You can always spot a rank amateur when he remarks, "Uh-oh. This is bad!" In fact, there are very few purely "bad" indications in any writing. The "bad" comes from *how* the writer uses his personality traits and you must look at the combination of the signs in the entire writing sample to tell you that. A HANDWRITING ANALYSIS SHOULD NEVER FOCUS ON ONE STROKE IN THE SCRIPT AND AN ABRUPT JUDGMENT MADE.

Consequently, for an analysis to reflect a truly reliable expression of an individual's personality, the traits are gathered from the whole sample of writing, from the size, slant, speed, pressure, letter formations and others. These are then compared, their strengths and weaknesses evaluated and their frequency considered.

Professional graphologists tackle a written sample armed with an array of helpful instruments and techniques: measuring devices, magnifying glasses, graphs and charts listing many personality traits. Skillfully applied, the graphologist is able to unveil the wondrous spectrum of uniqueness that identifies the true, individual self.

Charlie Cole, founder of the American Handwriting Analysis Foundation, is known for his successful work in personnel selection through graphology. Figure 1 is his worksheet for evaluating the occupational personality of a professional secretary.

While an in-depth study of graphology can be a fascinating adventure, the modern businessman has neither the time nor inclination, and that's not the purpose of this book. On the pages that follow, Traitmatch shows you a simple, highly practical way to apply graphology in business, bridging the gap between a detailed science and a sorely needed reliable selection process. You will learn other valuable uses as well, such as office compatibility, money skills and health signs, how to pick potential leaders and expose potential thieves.

No longer is industry interested only in the mechanical functions when evaluating the particular requirements for a job; personality traits are considered just as critical. The U.S. Department of Labor encourages the use of personality traits for job selection as shown in Figure 2. See Page 20.

Some administrators, distraught over the poor results from biased interviewing and inadequate personality testing, have tried other hiring and placement ideas.

One popular concept is to hire on "proven abilities" and not on the basis of personality traits. But the horse, even in these modern times, must come before the cart. Proven skills spring from a blend of traits already existing in the personality. Past performance is certainly one important hiring indicator, but kicking an employee upstairs or hiring fresh blood on proven abilities alone risks invoking the Peter Principle, and some outstanding supervisor will be promoted to the level of incompetent executive.

Look at the specific job traits required, then find the prospect's traits using the reliable tool of graphology.

Whether you are an executive of a large firm or the owner of a small business, this book will give you the means of locating the

SECRETARIES PERSONALITY CRITERIA

Name _____ For _____

I. INTELLIGENCE	____	**VII. LEADERSHIP** ____
Common sense	____	Will power ____
Reasoning power	____	Positivism ____
Intuition & insight	____	Forceful & dynamic ____
Analytical	____	Flair for dramatic ____
Flexibility	____	Ego drives ____
II. INDEPENDENCE	____	**VIII. HUMAN RELATIONS** ____
Self regimented	____	Friendliness ____
Self confidence	____	Responsiveness ____
Self control	____	Enthusiasm ____
Self respect	____	Non-critical ____
Self starter	____	Diplomacy ____
III. EMOTIONAL STABILITY	____	**IX. CONTROLLED INITIATIVE** ____
Reliability	____	Natural fighter ____
Self knowledge	____	Aggressiveness ____
Tension relaxation	____	Dominance need ____
Parental oriented	____	Urge to win ____
Natural spontaneity	____	Superiority drive ____
IV. PERFORMANCE	____	**X. COMMUNICATION** ____
Details	____	Emotionally empathic ____
Memory	____	Suggestivity ____
Follow through	____	Understandable ____
Compliance	____	Verbal facility ____
Financial facility	____	Uses reason ____
V. PERSERVERANCE & RESILIENCE	____	**XI. PHYSICAL & PSYCHIC ENERGIES** ____
Stick-to-it-iveness	____	Vitality & vigor ____
Determination	____	Activity compulsions ____
Integrity & ego-strength	____	Harnessed libido ____
Rebuff bounce back	____	Physical stamina ____
Work horse	____	Get up & go ____
VI. ORIGINALITY & CREATIVITY	____	
Progressiveness	____	
Resourceful spontaneity	____	
Ingenuity	____	
Conformity freedom	____	
Versatility & variety	____	

Figure 1

people who will make money for you. By analyzing their handwriting before you hire, your employees will benefit too, and be happier in jobs more suitable to their personalities.

If you're out of work now and looking for a job, or unhappy in your present work, you can apply the technique of Traitmatch to your own handwriting. Never again will you say, "This job just isn't me." It *will* be you, when you learn to use the simple method explained in this book.

Other Facts About Traitmatch

Age Age has traditionally been the means of judging mental maturity. Yet you've undoubtedly known mature teenagers and immature adults. Graphology reveals the manifestations of intellectual and emotional maturity, but doesn't—in fact, can't—identify the chronological age of the person. So unless you're hiring for a specific age group, knowledge of the applicant's age may be helpful.

Gender It's impossible to tell if a sample of writing came from a man or woman. However, the handwriting does reflect the personality traits which society labels as *masculine* or *feminine*.

From the moment of conception every human being begins life possessing the characteristics of both sexes. Eventually, the sex of the child is set, but each one of us has both male and female genes in our biological makeup. You've met *masculine* females and *feminine* males.

While masculine or feminine *qualities* can be found through graphology, the bias of whether they came from a man or a woman is eliminated.

In 1973, an experiment was conducted with 118 personnel managers.* They were asked to pick the factors for hiring a male white collar worker and a female white collar worker. The results were that the managers saw the man as an administrative management type (persuasive, aggressive, motivated), but the woman was perceived to be a typical clerical employee (pleasant voice, clerical and computational skills, immaculate in dress and person), clearly showing discrimination against women in management jobs.

---

*"Perceived Importance of Selected Variables used to evaluate Male and Female Job Applicants," Personnel Psychology, 1976 by Earl A. Cecil, Robert J. Paul and Robert A. Olins.

1. High level of responsibility
2. Competitive
3. Requires physical stamina
4. Works with detail
5. Work produces tangible product
6. Opportunity for self-expression
7. Generally confined to work area
8. Motivates others
9. Overtime or shift work required
10. Work is closely supervised
11. Directs activities of others
12. Exposed to weather conditions
13. Repetitious work
14. Helping people
15. Working with ideas
16. Working with people
17. Working with things
18. Works independently
19. Works as part of a team

Two extra spaces are provided for you to fill in the characteristics for other jobs you might be interested in.

Accountant
Advertising Worker
Agricultural Engineer
Architect
Automotive Mechanic
Barber
Carpenter
Cashier
Chef
Commercial Artist
Dental Assistant
Dentist
Draftsman
Electrician
Forester
Insurance Agent
Janitor
Machine Tool Operator
Meat Cutter
Mechanical Engineer
Medical Lab Technician
Nurse (RN)
Personnel Worker
Photographer
Physician
Plumber
Police Officer
Radio/TV Service Tech
Rehabilitation Counselor
Secretary
Social Worker
Statistician
Truck Driver
X-ray Technician
Other
Other

Figure 2
JOB PROFILE ANALYSIS CHART

The bias of gender choice can be eliminated by keeping knowledge of the applicant's sex from the Traitmatch analyst.

This isn't possible in job interviewing, obviously. It can even become more complicated. One personnel director interviewed a transvestite. What was the bias of the interviewer; against man, against woman, or against sexual variance? It could be this strangely-clad job seeker possessed the exact combination of skills or traits being sought by that company. A close look at the handwriting would have told.

Race and Religion The color of a person's skin or religious affiliation can't be determined through handwriting analysis, preventing more potential prejudices from influencing the hirer.

Nationality The subtle script variations between people of different national origins and those educated in a foreign country do not affect the handwriting enough to be significant.

Right or Left-handed? What happens when accident or paralysis causes a permanent switch to another hand? Or is there a difference between the writing of a right-handed or left-handed person?

Professor Aron E. Kobrinsky, doctor of Engineering at the USSR Academy of Sciences and his colleagues developed an artificial arm which operates electronically to perform as a real hand does, using impulses from the brain.

Electrodes are implanted on the ends of nerves which would ordinarily move arm muscles. When the stump has healed and the prosthesis fitted, the impulses coming from the brain are amplified and routed to the artificial arm, providing the stimuli for relays to operate.

Within the last few years a variation to this device known as a myoelectric prosthesis has been marketed, utilizing receptors attached to the skin rather than surgically implanted. The person writing with an artificial arm uses the same graphological signs as he did before the amputation. Other handicapped persons have exhibited the same writing tendencies holding a pen with their teeth, lips or toes! Not only does this show how little difference it makes if a person is right or left-handed, it illustrates remarkable evidence that handwriting is really "brainwriting." The same brain guides all members of the body and the uniqueness of personality flows onto the paper. The skill may be less in some cases, but the basic formations are there nevertheless.

21

Try this experiment: write with the hand you don't normally use. If you're right-handed, write for a few minutes with your left hand. If you're left-handed, write down a few sentences with your right. It will be awkward at first, but soon you will find the script will closely resemble your normal writing.

I usually write with my right hand.

Right handed

I usually write with my right hand.

Left handed

This writer is normally right handed. Notice that the awkward example written with the left hand still reflects many of the same letter forms.

The capital I is printed. The second word "usually" has no beginning stroke while the two "w" words in both examples do have beginning strokes. The "y" in "my" has no loop. The "g" in "right" resembles a figure 8 in both examples. Notice also that the breaks between letters occur in the same place in both right and left-handed examples.

The awkward picture of the left-handed example is the most obvious difference. Also the different slants of the downstrokes and the left influence attached to the *t* crosses and *i* dots. All these factors show why the analyst needs to know the handedness of the writer. The mechanics of pushing the pen (with the left hand) or pulling the pen (with the right hand) to form the letter are different. When a depth analysis is made, extra emphasis is applied to these factors for the writing of a left-handed person.

Chapter 2
HOW TO START

"You should use every profitable tool available for your business. Handwriting analysis is another method of personnel selection and evaluation. In fact, a number of courts in various states have accepted expert testimony from graphologists. I recently gave a seminar to a group of attorneys who were interested in using it for jury selection."

Jean Calori smiled at the gentleman seated across from her. Frank Evans studied the graphologist a moment, leaned back and pushed a flame into the bowl of his pipe.

"You'd make a pretty good lawyer yourself, Mrs. Calori," he grinned. *"You've been giving me a pretty convincing argument. But do you mind if I reserve some doubt about your claim of its effectiveness?"*

Jean Calori laughed. "Objection sustained! Seriously, I don't blame you for being cautious. You didn't reach your position here by making any rash decisions. However, each day that you don't use Traitmatch to select employees, you risk wasting time and money."

"What do you suggest?"

"Simply try it. This will be one time when your company will profit without an initial outlay of an arm and leg plus half of the company stock. In fact, the only cost will be the time it takes to learn the technique of Traitmatch."

Frank Evans adjusted his desk blotter, aligning it carefully with the mahogany edge. He looked up. "We use multiple personality inventories here as a selection device. Couldn't I have my people evaluate this handwriting analysis procedure by giving it a try along with the personality testing?"

"Certainly," agreed Jean, *"—but that's already been done. The most recent comparison was performed for a large Porche-Audi dealer in the midwest and..."*

"The results concurred?" Frank Evans interrupted.

"Yes," Jean nodded. *"Except the results from the handwriting analysis were found to be MORE satisfactory than their routine testing procedures. The graphologist who made the selection studies later became a regular part of the company's hiring procedure."*

Frank Evans nodded, impressed. *"Okay, Mrs. Calori,"* he said, *"We'll try Traitmatch for a while, then take another look at our turnover rate."* He reflamed his pipe, adding, *"How do I start putting Traitmatch to work?"*

By definition, Traitmatch is *discovering the occupational personality through handwriting analysis, selecting the most suitable employee by matching the more obvious personality traits found in the handwriting of job applicants to the personality traits required for a specific job.*

Just as there are no two personalities exactly alike, there are no two jobs which call for identical traits. Any specific job will change from time to time as responsibilities and work is shifted. Therefore, no job description can be an absolute. There is no standard formula. You, the employer, must decide. In larger organizations, a job analyst continually updates the duties of a particular position; working conditions, amount of pay, as well as the effects on training and promotion.

This inevitable evolution of job duties has its effect on a company staff. Only one in every 900 employees will stay for more than ten years. Developing businesses expect these internal changes. Static job analyses could signal a wilting corporate flower.

To use Traitmatch effectively, you must:

1. List the personality traits the job requires. It may be helpful to further evaluate the degree of use of each characteristic—a heavy emphasis, moderate or slight degree of desirability of the personality trait;

2. Compare the various personality traits found in the handwriting of job applicants. If a sign indicating a personality trait is found once or twice per page, it's only a clue that the characteristic is there. A frequently used sign, however, represents a developed trait. Excessive use of the same sign

reveals a highly developed talent, when it appears in a script that's pleasing to the eye. In an awkward handwriting, it denotes an obsession.

3. Hire the employee whose personality traits most closely match those required for the specific job.

To illustrate, notice the different personality traits required for an over-the-counter sales clerk working at a department store and a sales representative selling to large businesses. Both deal with people. Both sell. But the traits required for success in each job vary.

Sales Clerk	Sales Representative
Indoor person	Outdoor person
Sense of humor (moderate)	Sense of humor (strong)
Ambition (moderate)	Ambition (strong)
Friendly (strong)	Showmanship (moderate)
Patience (strong)	Verbal expression (strong)
Sympathetic (moderate)	Enthusiastic (strong)
Physical endurance (moderate)	Self-starter (strong)
Pursuasive	Persistent

The sales clerk has customers coming to him. Sometimes he needs to convince a hesitant customer of his need for the product. Standing behind the counter all day takes stamina. A cheerful disposition and sense of humor helps.

On the other hand, the sales representative must sell his own personality before he can even show his product to a customer. He therefore needs a strong sense of self-reliance and enthusiasm. The sales representative must be able to express himself easily yet not earbang or oversell his clients.

Once you've described the job in terms of personality traits required, you are ready to find and match the personality traits of the job applicants.

The Handwriting Sample

For an accurate analysis of handwriting, a good sample is necessary. It can be obtained by having the prospective employee, while filling out the job application, write two additional pages in his own handwriting telling why he wants to work for you.

This accomplishes three things. It enables you to find out how much the applicant actually knows about your business; it demonstrates his ability to express his thoughts; and you get a good sample of writing.

The best handwriting sample is written on an unlined 8½" × 11" sheet of paper, so a couple of sheets of regular typing paper will suit your needs perfectly.

You may even tell the applicant his writing will be analyzed, but this is apt to make him less spontaneous.

Most people begin to write in a careful manner, writing slower than their usual speed, forming letters with caution. As the writer relaxes, more attention is placed on *what* is written rather than on *how* it is written. This is the reason you should always ask for two pages. Lay aside the first page and concentrate on the second page for your analysis. By the time the applicant has written that first page he has relaxed enough to write the second page with the speed and spontaneity that's natural for him. His writing will then indeed be the "frozen self-image" that the psychologists Vernon and Allport called handwriting in their classic book, "Studies In Expressive Movements".

What About Printing?

The need for clarity in the business world is the first thing emphasized by companies to prospective employees. The top of the job application states, "PRINT—DON'T WRITE".

Printing, however, is not comfortable for every writer. In Traitmatch, the employer understands this and requests the applicant to "WRITE OR PRINT IN YOUR NATURAL HAND-WRITING".

While printing is analyzed much the same as cursive writing (also known as "longhand"), there are some general differences in the personalities involved. Unlike the cursive writer who is more oriented to ideas, feelings and people, the habitual printer is pragmatic, thinking in a detailed, objective manner. He sees life as a series of small fragments that can be pieced together to form a whole.

The person who claims that he can print faster than he can write usually means he is more familiar with printing and that his thinking processes are more tuned to the rhythm and speed found in printing. Therefore, he's naturally more comfortable with this type of coordination between hand and brain.

You will discover by learning and using Traitmatch that printing can have positive and negative connotations, depending on other signs found in the writing. A printer can be a fantasizer living in a dream world of his own design or have conflict fitting the fragments of life together. Another printer fits them together nicely and uses them to complete his projects as does the draftsman, data processor and architect. More about printing in Chapter 10.

The Basic Factors of Graphology

There are five basic factors of graphology the Traitmatch analyst will be using to pick the right person for the right job. They are: SLANT, SPACING, PRESSURE, SPEED AND CLARITY.

SLANT

Letter Slant = Emotional Response.
Letter slant can best be seen in letters containing upper loops; the b, d, h, l, k, and t. The more the letter slant leans toward the right, the more emotional response can be expected.

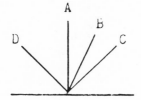

A = self-reliant, independent
B = compliant, outgoing
C = emotional, garrulous
D = reserved, cold, withdrawn

Most people write with a slight right slant (B). This shows a willingness to comply with company rules, an ability to get along with co-workers, and put up with the boss's idiosyncracies.

Writers with an extreme right slant can function well on the job, but might become hysterical under sudden emotional stress.

27

Extreme left-slanted writers are sometimes antisocial, non-communicative, even defiant at times.

Baseline Slant = Goal Directiveness

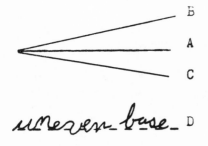

A = good goal direction
B = optimism
C = pessimism, fatigue
D = moody, restless

Writing "uphill" reveals the applicant worthy of further Trait-match evaluation. He's optimistic, ambitious and cheerful. This is a good start, and, if the other traits bear up well under your scrutiny, a welcome addition to any office force or gang crew.

Writing "downhill" may be caused by a temporary depression, ill health, or physical fatigue. If this applicant has special skills necessary in your business, it would be wise to have him return on another day and obtain another sample of his writing. The first downslanted sample could be just a temporary discouragement from job-hunting. If the second sample has the same downslanted appearance, it is a warning of an ingrained pessimism which keeps this applicant on the job-seeking circuit.

The writer of a firm, straight, even baseline controls his moods, allowing him to go directly toward his goals without getting side-tracked.

While a very slight wave in the baseline is a common sign, an unusual up-and-down fluctuation identifies the moody individual. A ruler placed under the first and last letters in a line of writing is an excellent way to determine an uneven baseline. Be sure you need this person's talents desperately before hiring him. He may be a go-getter on his "up" days, but if he's in a "downer" mood, he probably won't even show up for work.

More baseline variations can be found in Chapter 9, "Hieroglyphics of Health".

SPACING

Spaces in writing are just as important to the Traitmatch analyst as the writing itself. Spaces are found around the whole page of writing (the margin); in the amount of room that the letters take up (the letter size); in the generous or compressed usage of space between letters, lines, and words. All offer many clues to detect the occupational personality.

A general rule-of-thumb is that the way in which a person uses space when writing indicates his use of space in his work.

Check the application form. How did the prospect use the spaces within the blanks, boxes, or fill-ins? If he crowded the letters to the left, he's fearful of his future. If he pushed all the letters to the right, he's ambitious and eager for the job. If he couldn't contain his writing within the spaces provided, he's not a good judge of time and space. More about revelations on the job application in Chapter 10, "The Square Crystal Ball."

Margin = Attitude Toward Environment

The position of the writing on a page within a margin frame shows how the potential employee regards his position or "space" within the company framework.

PICTURE FRAME MARGIN (even, well-defined) =

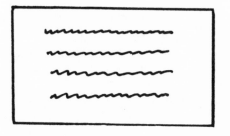

aware of space and time
artistic, good taste
aesthetic

Traitmatch for*: art-related and clerical occupations and public servants.

WIDE LEFT MARGIN (narrow right margin) =

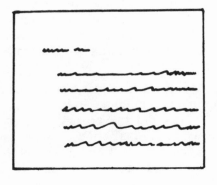

interest in future
ambition
socially oriented

Traitmatch for: jobs having opportunity for advancement, **sales** promotional worker, receptionist, hostess.

NARROW LEFT MARGIN (wide right margin) =

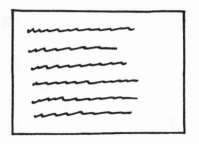

interest in past
works best behind scenes
introspective

Traitmatch for: historian, researcher, stock clerk, production analyst, computer programmer.

Letter Size = Ego.

Every letter takes up space, too. Some letters extend into the upper area of the writing and are referred to as upper-zone letters: *b*, *d*, *h*, *k*, *l*, and *t*. The lower-zone letters are the *g*, *j*, *p*, *q*, *y*, and *z*. Most letters are found in the middle zone of writing. The size of the middle zone is the major factor considered in handwriting analysis. Almost all other signs are compared to it.

f is the only letter that reaches all three zones.

Large writing and small writing refers to the middle-zone size, and are both easy to spot. Most people's script falls somewhere in between, however. This "average size" of writing is found in the sample of applicants who can fit into almost any kind of job situation for which they are qualified. Their uniqueness will be revealed in other writing features.

Large writing indicates a person who will need plenty of space in which to operate. Don't try to put him behind a desk or in any small confining area.

LARGE MIDDLE ZONE (large writing) =

> demand for attention
> need for elbow room

large writing

Traitmatch for: outdoor work (construction, conservation), canvassing, door-to-door selling, agricultural work.

Small writing reveals the individual willing to work behind the scenes. This writer can also stick with a detailed job for long periods of time.

SMALL MIDDLE ZONE (small writing) = reserved
                                    intelligent
                                    modest, unassuming
                                    ability to concentrate
                                    non-spotlight job

Dear Mrs. Whiting,
Just a short note

Traitmatch for: bookkeeper, researcher, statistician, computer analyst, systems writer.

Upper-Zone Extensions = Philosophy of Life
   The upper zone of writing holds the philosophy of life. It contains the writer's thought patterns including his ability to utilize abstract thinking in his daily routine.
   Most people push their letters to a moderate height into the upper zone showing their ability to think clearly about practical things. This writer fits nicely into a job where concrete ideas are required, as long as they are not too technical.

TALL UPPER-ZONE EXTENSIONS =
                              abstract thinker
                              intellect
                              philosophical mind

tall letters

Traitmatch for: ministers, advertising skills, psychologists, executives.

   Short upper-zone extensions are made by the writer who has short term goals, and is not idea-oriented.

SHORT UPPER-ZONE EXTENSIONS =

> practical, down-to-earth
> mechanical
> short-term goals

short

Traitmatch for: mechanical and manual occupations, assembly line work.

Lower-Zone Extensions = Physical and Sexual Drives

The prospective employee's interest in physical activity is the primary interest of many companies. The lower-zone extensions reflect the applicant's physical and sexual activity, as well as his concern for money and food.

Large, full lower loops, especially when they extend far below the baseline, are made by the person who wants to live life to the fullest.

LARGE LOWER LOOPS =

> extreme physical drive
> sensual
> hungry
> active

large loops

Traitmatch for: sexual surrogate, amateur or professional sports, wine taster, food critic, cook.

Long lower loops disclose the person needing plenty of physical space.

33

LONG LOWER LOOPS =

strong physical drive

long lower zone

Traitmatch for: warehouseman, lumberjack, heavy equipment operators, jazzercizer, waiter, marathon runner.

Short lower loops expose the individual entirely disinterested in physical activity.

SHORT LOWER LOOPS =

disinterested in physical
possible laziness
sedentary

*cry your
ing four*

Traitmatch for: mattress tester, reader, quilter.

"NON-LOOPS" (lower-zone extensions resembling sticks) =

stoicism
simple tastes
gets the job done

graphology

Traitmatch for: Hotel desk clerk, parking lot attendants, typists, camper, fisherman.

Extreme Expansion = Self-Expansion.
Expansion is the horizontal extension of letters and space, presenting a stretched appearance.

EXTREME EXPANSION =

need for room
generosity
freedom from supervision
(works best alone)
entrepreneur

expansion

Traitmatch for: independent thinkers, sales persons, executives.

Extreme Compression = Self-Limitation.
Compression is the squeezing of letters, words and spaces.

EXTREME COMPRESSION =

introversion
ability to work in small spaces
the office "tightwad"

compression

Traitmatch for: radio disc jockeys, control room technicians, bookkeeper, librarian, loan officer, budget director, treasurer.

Spaces Between Lines = Capacity For Thought Organization.

LINES SEPARATED, EVENLY SPACED =

clear thought
able to organize work

Seems good ?

back to take over

don't feel up to m

Traitmatch for: contractors, planners, organizers, executives, interior decorator.

LINES CROWDED TOGETHER, OVERLAPPING LOOPS =
confused thinking
poor organization of time and space
overly familiar

Traitmatch for: junk dealer, supply yard worker, swap meet worker.

Spacing Between Words

Spacing between words should be about the same width as the middle-zone letters. If spacing is consistent, it adds to the possibility of the writer being consistent. It is a positive trait for any job.

socially adjusted
able to meet the public

Traitmatch for: real estate agent, hostess, receptionist, waiter, public relations.

PRESSURE

Pressure measures the degree of intensity the employee will put into his work as well as his physical vitality and stamina. For instance, poets, speakers, politicians and ministers often have heavier writing pressure because they put emotion into what they have to say.

The type of pen used will have some effect on the pressure. The soft-tipped pen can conceal the light-pressured writer. The Traitmatch analyst can tell this by turning the paper over and running his fingers over the back of the writing surface. If you feel or see the embossing caused by pressure from the pen, you

36

are assured that the writer was using a ball point, not a soft-tipped pen and the pressure is genuine.

Pressure takes a certain amount of physical exertion, and the soft-tipped pen user enjoys the easy flow of ink over the page. Soft-tipped pens are a cop-out for physical labor. However, they are also used by artists and sensual people. Check with other Traitmatch signs to determine if the writer is lazy.

HEAVY PRESSURE =

I hate to see you do this !

intense emotions
strong sensual needs
good health
strong vitality
realistic

Traitmatch for: heavy machine operator, outdoor worker, fire-fighter, police, poet, polician, minister.

MEDIUM PRESSURE =

perceptive
good memory
conservative

dear Miss Whiting.

Traitmatch for: tellers, statitician, executive secretary.

LIGHT PRESSURE =

gentle, cultural
avoids confrontation
sedentary
prefers intellectual approach

much I am
Roger Wagner
Singing Youth

Traitmatch for: non-stress jobs, telephone solicitors, music li-brarian, orchid grower, court reporter.

SPEED

Speed is found in the flow of the writing and indicates speed of thought, action and perception. Additionally, writing that has few or no beginning strokes shows the stripping away of unnecessary details contributing to the applicant's efficiency in getting the job done.

Note the T-crosses. If the cross is longer on the right side of the stem than on the left side, the writer is hurrying to complete his simple task of crossing the *t*. I-dots which fall to the right of the stem also indicate speed.

FAST WRITING =

the best beloved in my sight

alertness
perceptiveness
flexibility
maturity
rapid thinker

Traitmatch for: any job requiring fast thinking, supervisor, exective, pilot, caterer, journalist, TV performer.

SLOW WRITING =

slow thinker
delibrate
cautious thinker
precision

I am not in a hurry.

Traitmatch for: watchmaker, craftsman, inventor, researcher.

CLARITY

Clarity involves all of the basic factors of handwriting analysis in a positive way. It's a good idea to keep in mind that when clarity in a written sample is combined with—
• A slight, right slant = interest in communicating with others;

- Medium size writing = willingness to contact others physically and mentally.
- Balanced expansion = reaching out to become involved.
- Even margins = good sense of self-identity within the environment.
- Good spacing between letters = generosity of time, money energy.
- Good spacing between words = interest in social contacts.
- Good space between lines = ability to think clearly and separate ideas.
- Clear formation of letters = wish to impart information and consideration for others.

Illegible writing, whether scribbled by a world-wise scientist or by your inexperienced job applicant, indicates the individual who doesn't have the time or inclination to communicate.

Someone once mentioned that the less legible the writing, the more intelligent the writer. Ever since then, some people have hidden their laziness and inconsideration behind that remark.

One secretary complained, "My boss is such a terrible writer I can hardly make out what he means. Last week he didn't read over a letter before he signed it and I had typed something all wrong. I got bawled out. I think it was his fault, don't you?"

You bet! But secretaries aren't the only ones who suffer. Ask your local pharmacist, for instance.

Illegible script is the curse of good communication, and writing is—first and foremost—communication.

Many bosses have an executive type of mind; sharp, alert, quick. But the employer who doesn't take the time or effort to make his written thoughts clear enough to be translated by a secretary or anyone else is both inconsiderate and lacking in common sense.

Speed is the prime offender. We think faster than our fingers can move. Unless control is exercised over both thoughts and fingers, the results are usually unreadable.

A good secretary can sometimes guess what the boss means by the general shape of the word, plus the context of the statement, but not always. And few secretaries can read minds.

There are, however, other reasons for illegibility in handwriting. It may be caused by emotional stress or an illness resulting in muscular impairment or hysteria. Also, a dishonest person hides his intentions behind poor writing.

39

Illegibility may be caused by more serious reasons than speed or inconsideration. When the physical or mental vitality of a writer is impaired through the use of drugs or alcohol, illegible writing is often a result. The uneven baseline is usually the first clue, signaling the lack of motor control. Letters not clearly formed due to speed may occur in every writing at any time, but when a sequence of letters fails to make sense, there is more than speed or inconsistency at work. If this is repeated on a page or two of writing, drop that application in the round file. You don't need the problems that can be brought to your workplace by this kind of employee.

Ill health often shows up in illegible writing especially if the writing also has weak pressure. There just is not enough vitality there for the writer to get through a good day's work. However, we all have our off days. If all other factors are favorable, and you might like to have him on your work team, suggest he come back another time to repeat his writing sample. Chapter 9 deals with this subject in more detail.

Dishonesty is another thing entirely. We have devoted Chapter 7 to honesty and dishonesty. Strength of will and courageous moral fibre makes the difference between an honest and a dishonest person, yet timing, opportunity and health often have as much to do with dishonesty in business as do weak will or poor moral standards.

Chapter 3
TRAITMATCHING INTELLIGENCE

In Idaho Falls, Idaho, a model welfare program was developed. In an effort to help mentally retarded adults through work therapy, thirty-one individuals were trained to turn pieces of wood into survey stakes. These were sold to businesses throughout the state. The new employees were so well suited to their jobs that the program began to show a nice profit.

Ironically, the success of these mentally restricted workers brought about their occupational demise. No administrative mechanism existed to accommodate a welfare program that actually made money. The project was abandoned.

The Cerebral Enigma

Misplaced brains continue to be a major cause of high turn-over rates. Discovering the job applicant is a mental whiz doesn't insure the dawn of a successful career. Higher intellect. usually thought to be a prime asset can be a handicap as well.

Yet the phrase, "He's smart. We can use him..." still exists in the strange world of the hiring hassle. A job candidate is often picked for the single quality of intelligence. Of course, being "smart" implies more than merely the ability to retain academic knowledge. It describes a person with that marvelous blend of qualities which give him the ability to perceive the wide scope of this company's goals and relate his job to them, including his talent to *apply* that knowledge to solving problems, meeting and adjusting to the new challenges life brings.

When an economic rollback results in a purge of a large corporation, such as those made in recent years by the aircraft industry, an already crowded job market becomes more saturated by highly intelligent people; scientists, engineers, executives. Unable to find work in fields in which he is qualified, this new breed of job seeker is forced to hunt for employment demanding much less of his mental skills.

To skirt around impressive but unwanted credentials, the puzzling phrase "over-qualified" began to slide off corporate tongues. Rather than encouraged or placated with this label, the job seeker is left perplexed. If he's such a hot-shot, why is he still out in the snow?

The reason is that companies have learned hiring mental giants for work that's routine and repetitive, the kind of job that once learned seems to progress almost by itself, usually spells disaster. But Ph. D's and others with stately credentials conceal their qualifications and are placed into disappointing jobs they will soon leave.

On the flip side of the intellectual scale, an employee thrust into a complex job beyond his mental capacity is soon fired or he quickly makes his own exit, on his way no doubt to the welfare office or a psychiatrist's couch.

It's enough to make gray matter turn blue.

But don't despair. Like the Idaho Falls experiment demonstrated, every level of mentality has a place in business if job and individual are properly matched. How? Follow the trail of the pen!

For eighteen months Irv Perch, chief executive officer and founder of the Aristocrat chain of recreational vehicles, had been struggling with production managers. After hiring three, all of whom possessed managerial degrees, business was still sluggish.

Perch kept his eye open for new blood within his company. One of his employees had been born in Spain and could neither read nor write much English. He ran away from school at about fourth grade level and worked his way across the ocean, across Canada, and finally into the midwest where he became a sheepherder. Perch had hired him mainly to help him to communicate with the Mexicans in the manufacturing shop. Perch approached the graphologist Charliè Cole and asked him to check the Spaniard's ability to handle one of the five crews in the shop.

After his analysis of the employee's handwriting, Charlie reported to Perch. "This man has more practical intelligence than your three fellows with degrees. Never mind trying him out with one crew. I suggest you give him all five crews. He can handle the men and you can trust him with your business."

Somewhat dubious, Perch took Cole's advice. The Spaniard has been running the shop successfully for over three years, supervising 140 men with a substantial increase in production.

The bottom line is this: present hiring methods do little to solve the cerebral enigma; the inadequate placement of intellect. But traitmatching for intelligence can help you find the right person for the job. Unfortunately, no single squiggle or swirl captures the quality of intelligence, but it's there! An intelligent person is said to be objective and organized, maintaining a comfortable balance between mental flexibility and control. He may think in a logical or intuitive manner and his memory serves him well. By evaluating the basic handwriting signs for these specific mental skills, you can discover the person whose thinking cap is screwed on tight and right.

Script Simplification and IQ

The relationship of intelligence to simplified writing is perhaps the most universally accepted of all graphological signs. Research has found that people with relatively high intellect simplify their handwriting more than do those of average intellect.

Simplification doesn't refer to the copy-book stroking of a school child. It pertains to the written result of any action a writer uses to make the act of writing easier (simpler) for himself. This often means a *departure* from the way the writer was taught, while keeping the script legible in the process.

One of the most common ways to save time and energy while writing is to shorten the beginning strokes of a word, or drop them entirely. Words may also be ended abruptly, without the addition of a final appendage or "tail." Watch for this lack of excess baggage.

Simplified beginning and final strokes

43

and seven years
ght forth upon t

Compare this copybook style

The Figure 8

Often original and intelligent writers will create "short-cut" strokes as they simplify, indicating their ingenuity in handling problems. The figure 8 is one of these. Normally found in place of the letter *g*, it can appear anywhere in the script. Note in this sample, for example, the *s* also has the appearance of a figure 8.

hen (graduate school years
(something for

figure 8's

In a study by Epstein, Hartford and Tumarkin, the figure 8 *g* correlated higher with educational level, IQ and age than any other single letter variant studied.* However, any sign of simplifying or economizing in the script is indicative of greater intellectual maturity.

Objectivity

Thought is constantly influenced by preferences. We can never get away from our own personal likes and dislikes. They are bound to creep into our thinking processes and color our decisions. Since it's impossible to remove all traces of emotional involvement, you should traitmatch for minimal distortion of

---

*For a more detailed discussion of this experiment, see Huntington Hartford's "You Are What You Write" (Macmillan).

personal feelings or prejudices. The more objectivity found, the greater will be the quality of intellectual utility.

Four signs of objectivity are: open ovals; good spacing between letters, words and lines; vertical writing, and clean, simple strokes.

Open ovals indicate openess of mind; the willingness to accept new ideas. But it's rare to find a writing with *all* of the oval letters open at the top. In fact, it's not desirable either, for any excess is apt to result in the negative use of a quality that would otherwise be positive. So look for a balance of open ovals with a few others that are neatly tied without being elaborately knotted. This shows a blend between accepting new ideas without discrimination and confidence in one's own convictions.

Ovals in balance

Spacing between words, lines and letters reveals the writer who gives himself space to think, free from superfluous mental clutter which sometimes gets in the way of direct thought. Good judgment as well as objectivity spring from the writer who utilizes good proportion between space and size in his script. Vertical writing strengthens evaluation for objectivity because the writer is freer from emotional influences than the slanted writer. Clean, simple strokes indicates his ideas are well-defined.

Objective writing

45

Organizational Abilities

To be put to effective use, intelligence must include organizational abilities. An organized mind is capable of systemizing a collection of facts and information.

While an orderly system and arrangement are implied in organization, meticulous neatness and rigid order could hamper the process, so a certain freedom and fluency are required in the best samples of organized writing.

Look for orderly distribution in all five of the basic factors— slant, spacing, pressure, clarity and speed.

Organized writing is also consistant in slant and firmness of pressure. The writing is not stiff, however, and moves fluently across the page. Check the margins to see if they are well-defined and relatively uniform. You should be able to read the words easily.

The Organized f

One of the quickest ways to check organization potential is to note the balance of the upper loops with the lower loops. Look particularly for the letter *f,* the only letter in the alphabet which incorporates all three zones of writing. Even distribution of the upper and lower loops of the *f* hints strongly of organizational abilities.

While this trait is an important one for executives, it can also be found in the script of the secretary who keeps a neat, efficient filing system or in the handwriting of an employee who organizes his time well and keeps appointments promptly.

the organized *f*

The Power To Reason

After you have determined that your job candidate has intelligence by checking the simplification, objectivity and organization in his writing, you'll want to know *how* he thinks. To consider him for that special job, you will need to understand whether the writer is a logical or intuitive thinker. We usually think of logic as a masculine trait and intuition as a femine quality. Actually, we all use some of both with one or the other dominating the personality.

The Logical Thinker

Logic involves a cause-and-effect reasoning in the effort to tackle life's problems. A logical person connects his letters as well as his thoughts. Letters consistently connected within long words reveals the writer who can hold a thought or a collection of ideas long enough to evaluate the end result. He builds one idea from the previous one, connecting a set of facts before coming to a logical conclusion.

The break between capital letters and the rest of the word, however, is a learned action from school and should not be considered a significant trait of the logical thinker. Even a logical thinker may occasionally disconnect letters within a word, but connected words of six letters or more is a strong indication of a logical thinker.

Consistent pressure is another sign of the logical thinker. Alfred Mendel in his book "Personality in Handwriting" states that a "reasonable pressure pattern in a script seems to me the most evident manifestation of the writer's acceptance of the laws of reason and order and his striving for logic, self-discipline and self-preservation within this reason and order."

The opposite sign, uneven pressure, immediately signals inconsistency, and with inconsistency, logic and reason dissolve.

Of course, an herb is for specific reasons - subtle catalyst or as

Connected writing with "reasonable pressure"

The Intuitive Thinker

The intuitive thinker takes thinking short-cuts. He writes with a series of disconnected words, skipping his pen across the paper. This person's quick insight often enables him to tote up high batting averages for accuracy as he mentally leaps, almost subconsciously, to conclusions. The intuitive thinker is willing

47

to play his hunches, take risks and gamble on a "feeling" that a certain course should be followed or action taken.

Disconnections are usually found after syllables, after capitals, and when the breaks afford the writer an opportunity to dot the *i* or cross the *t,* completing those letters before continuing the rest of the word. Breaks may also be found preceeding oval letters (the *o, a, d* and *g).*

When you find words with less than six letters containing two or more breaks, you have an intuitive thinker whose hunches could add zest and profit to your business.

Disconnected, intuitional writing

Depending on your individual job needs, the logical thinker and the intuitive thinker can be valuable contributors to your business. So traitmatch for the type best suited for your employment needs. For example, the handwriting of a successful submarine captain revealed a high degree of intelligence coupled with intuitive thought; an effective combination for a man who must make split-second decisions without the luxury of contemplation.

Flexibility and Control

Every company has its corporate personality formed by the individual personalities of those who work there. Your new employee must be able to adapt his own personality to your mental menagerie to be content and do a good job for you.

But too much flexibility reveals an applicant who will be apathetic, wishy-washy; lacking enough control and self-discipline to finish a job. You should seek out a nice balance between flexibility and control.

Look first for the garland (curved) type of writing with a right slant. This suggests the writer who hangs loose enough to roll with the punches when he encounters conflict in his new job.

Then look for the control that comes through good connections (for logic, right?), an even baseline and a good pressure to

48

indicate backbone. You will then have some of the ingredients which make up an intelligent employee.

Another nice find is slightly pointed *m*'s and *n*'s which show the ability for sharp, independent thinking rather than automatic blind obedience.

feel even a greater desire

Flexibility With Control

Note: There is also the garland writer who does not slant rightward. The writing may be vertical or left-slanted. This writer is flexible too, but only on his own terms. He will go along at first. Eventually he tends to adapt the environment to his ways rather than blending in with the corporate personality or social scenery.

is often that a child hits an accident or purposely done. Is want to be very calm and self and. If it is an accident, it

Garlands with vertical writing

Memory

Memory is the ability to store knowledge and experiences. Recall is greatly influenced by emotional involvement. We've all been able to quickly recall those things which meant the most to us; the fond remembrance of graduation, the cherished moment of a wedding proposal or executive promotion.

Samuel Johnson once remarked, ''The art of memory is the art of attention.'' Memory experts capitalize on this fact by focusing attention on the things they want to remember. So to find memory in handwriting, look for attention to detail. It's easy to find. Look for precisely dotted *i*'s, carefully placed *t*-crosses, and punctuation marks made with care. Small, legible script demonstrates graphically the concentration needed to write this style of script.

Since memory implies past experiences, we must find some connections to the past in the writing. Long beginning strokes links a writer to his copy-book days, hinting at a concern for the past. This writer may well have a better memory than the writer of simplified strokes, but whether he is remembering useful or superfluous data can't be readily seen.

Lastly, there should be enough emotional influence evident in the writing to insure a firm imprint on the mind. Depth of feeling is found in the writing pressure. One who feels deeply, remembering the details of past experiences, uses a medium or heavy pressure of good consistency.

Good pressure and attention to detail show a good memory.

A Rare Sense

You've seen how intelligence is comprised of simplification, objectivity and organization. You've learned to evaluate the additional intellectual dimensions of logic and intuition to discover the type of thought processes available to you through an applicant's writing. When you find flexibility and control in proper balance, you have that beautiful commodity known popularly as common sense.

But it's really not so common to find a person with all of these enviable mental characteristics after all. Such an applicant will truly have a "rare sense" of intelligence. Make a place for him in your business. He will definitely be worth his hire.

Chapter 4
LEADERSCRIPT

Realists in the business world agree that it's impossible for any one person to be endowed with all of the various traits desired in a leader. Executive head-hunter Richard Irish put it this way: "Nobody walks on water."

Among the most accepted and popular leadership characteristics are intelligence, self-esteem, communication adeptness, conceptual thinking, and decisiveness. For upper level management, psychologists add sociability, energy, emotional stability under pressure and cooperation.

You've learned how to traitmatch intelligence in Chapter Three. Conceptual thinking can be evaluated by combining the degree of originality found in the simplified script and the organizational ability. Now determine your prospect's confidence in himself to do the job.

The Confident Asset

Today, the job-seeker who presents a shy resume is doomed. Modesty is interpreted by personnel officers to be a lack of self-esteem. Many a managerial candidate has been deep-sixed by a meek display of his own past achievements or present skills.

On the other hand, the prospect who suffers from an exaggerated self-importance might not be able to acknowledge his limitations. But you can.

We were taught to make a capital *I* by beginning at the baseline, making a leftward loop, then returning to the baseline and up to the left, finishing with a horizontal line drawn to the right.

Copybook *I*

But few adults continue to use this learned style. They change once having adopted a self-image that they feel suits them.

Try this experiment. Ask your friends and business associates to write this sentence:

Ida and I went to Italy.

Compare the difference in the capital *I*'s, especially between the personal pronoun I and that used in the words *Ida* and *Italy.*

You'll be surprised at the variety.

The closer the capital *I* remains to the copybook style, the more conventional and conservative the writer regards himself.

Egotism is defined as excessive use of the first person singular. In graphology, egotism is identified by excessive *size* and *elaboration* of the first person singular. Letter size = ego, remember?

I am going to

Overconfident egotist

I decided

here, I hope you are

Self-conscious

52

The confident personality writes with a medium to large-sized script with firm pressure—without inflated or elaborated lettering. Vertical writing and rapid speed strengthen the signs of confidence.

I would like to know anything about me. might be revea analysis of my

The confident asset

The simplified capital *I* shows a writer who strips away superfluous thought and action. He is unconcerned about what other people think of him. A Roman numeral *I* is used by those who are constructive and independent. Stick-like *I*'s are indications of independence with cultural simplicity.

It seems I must have been

Roman numeral *I*

I know what I'm doing.

Stick-like *I*

Another clue to self-confidence is revealed in an underscored signature.

Self-confidence

The Ability to Communicate

Thomas V. Jones, chief executive officer for Northrop Corporation, heads up the aerospace company responsible for the fuselage of the Boeing 747 jumbo jet. Echoing the innermost feelings of most other CEO's he encourages easy communication in all levels of business: "The trick is to make everyone in the company aware."

Communication requires a willingness to reach out to others with a word, a look, or an expressive movement. It is the art of transmitting information, thought and emotions through outward expressions. We communicate through spoken or written words and by using body language. Knowledge is quickly imparted through smiles, frowns, throat clearings, giggles, gargles and groans.

The writer who communicates will show gracious garland-like connections between the letters of his words. He will often leave the a and o slightly open at the top, indicating a good command of the language and one who can "open up" with ease.

However, if all of the a's and o's are open, the writer is too open-mouthed; a chatter-box.

Ease with words

was exposed to

Ear-banger

Close Mouthed Boss

If all of the oval letters, the *a, o, d* and *g* are narrow and closed, the writer will appear to communicate but he will talk without really telling you what's on his mind. You can do without all this double-talk and extreme secretiveness in your business. For the amount of communication you'll receive from him, he may just as well be speaking pig latin.

*how he would
to help the a
he was hit.*

The secretive evader

Humor and Wit: Aids to Communication

While humor is not a requirement for communicating, it can help to pave the path to understanding, making the wheels of business life run smoother and happier. A welcome addition to any office staff or executive board is that person who skillfully alleviates an awkward situation with an amusing comment, a wry turn of a phrase or witty interjection.

Humor is detected in wavy beginning strokes, especially the capital *M* or *N*. An easy way to remember this sign is to think of the positions of the mouths on the twin masks of the theater, here symbolizing the ability to turn a frown into a smile:

Humor

Wit is humor with a bit more bite, jabbed home with a sharp mind. The witty writer also jabs his i-dots making them look like little tents. Tiny hooks can be found elsewhere in the writing. The humps of the *m*'s and *n*'s will contain sharp angles revealing the writer's acute mental ability to probe beyond the apparent.

It is said that th

spine is flexible

Wit

The Power to Make Decisions

The Roman historian Tacitus called leadership "reason and calm judgment." This seems as appropriate today as it was two thousand years ago. A decisive leader sets practical goals using his intelligence and objectivity. Making choices, particularly unpopular choices, and sticking to them is the mark of a true leader.

Determination

Strong downstrokes in the script, especially in the lower zone, signifies the physical activity and energy necessary to complete goals.

There are two kinds of "determined downstrokes." The unfinished downstroke, made with firm pressure indicates the person who can see a project through and doesn't waste precious time on extra frills or make a big production of it. He completes the necessary steps and moves on to the next task. This writer is not interested in the details. Just the nitty-gritty.

I am

currently

Determined time-saver

The completed lower loop made with a firm downstroke indicates a writer who takes the time to follow through on a project's unfinished details.

56

going through

Good follow-through

Firm t-crosses stroked over two or more letters to the right lends great purpose to the aims of the writer.

suggestions on this

Resoluteness

The Self-Starter
There are also decision-makers who can work well alone. This is the individual who can jump out of bed in the morning without being prodded by the alarm and needs no second cup of coffee to help pry him from the breakfast table and out the door. Seldom does he require a supervisor to push his starter button. As disgusting as he sounds to most of us, this rare bird does exist, and his writing has a look of speed and direction. His script will also be barren of beginning strokes.

Dear Mrs. Whiting,
I am very interested
my handwriting analyzed

The self-starter

Detriments to Decision-Making

Procrastination
If t-crosses don't quite make it through the stem but are made

57

with firm pressure, it indicates procrastination and is a common sign found in handwriting.

e, in due time,

Procrastination

Wishy-Washyness

Weak pressure in the writing may indicate a wishy-washy person, or one who is in poor health and doesn't have the necessary physical energy to carry out decisions.

In this weak-pressured writing if the t-crossings come up short it doesn't signify procrastination, but rather a fearfulness and lack of direction which hamper the writer's power to make decisions.

Additionally, the wishy-washy writer pens a somewhat flattened middle zone. The *m*'s and *n*'s fall away into a thin line. Words sometimes droop sadly to the right, exposing the personality who will have much difficulty withstanding the rigors of leadership.

teach in
q a master

Wishy-washy

Leadership is a quality that can be learned. Don't overlook the budding leader in your own corporate garden. If an employee has some of these positive talents in his writing and he already works for you, consider training him to your brand of leadership.

Chapter 5
OFFICE TOGETHERNESS

"The most widely approved personality in our culture is probably friendly and sociable, somewhat cooperative yet quite competitive and aggressively individualistic, progressive yet practical and efficient."
Horton and Hunt in SOCIOLOGY (McGraw-Hill, 1972)

From the blending of occupational personalities there emerges the company personality, an image flavored for the public taste. When hiring new employees or placing present staff, it's important to keep the company personality in mind, since changes will affect the office environment and utlimately the efficiency of personnel.

It's a good idea to determine the future goals of the job applicant. How far is he willing to utilize his energies to step up the promotional ladder? How effectively will he work with others? Does he work better alone? If you can avoid office conflicts before they occur by checking less than an ounce of his handwriting, it's worth more than a pound of cure.

Ambition

It's a fact of life that everyone wants something. Some want more than others. These "wants" might be called goals. But wanting something is not the only ingredient of ambition. There must also be a drive. Energy must be put forth toward achieving those goals.

Ambition in handwriting is found in rightward motions called *diagonals.* A diagonal is an upward stroke from left to right which indicates the writer's willingness to surge forward.

59

Diagonals can be found in all three zones of writing; in t-bars, in strokes used to complete some letters like the capital *H* and *F*. They are mostly found, however, in the up-strokes of the capital *M* and *N,* and in the upstrokes of lower zone loops.

Hello Mary Nixon

Diagonals

Upper Zone Diagonals

T-bars are found in the upper zone, the thinking area of writing. It signifies how the writer sets his goals and whether he will be able to follow through with them to completion. The length and pressure of the t-bar shows exactly how your candidate approaches his own personal goals. Less length and lighter pressure means less energy and enthusiasm. An enthusiastic, strongly ambitious t-bar should cover two or more letters and be made with an upswept diagonal.

High-goals: t-bar slanted
high on the stem

Practical goals: diagonal t-bar
halfway up the stem

Immediate goals only:
short t-bar immediately above
middle zone letters

Idealistic: Unattainable
goals. T-bar above stem.

Middle Zone Diagonals

The middle zone reflects practical action. Strong diagonals extending from the baseline of the middle zone show an energy reserve for use in day to day living. The ambitious person is often in a hurry to reach his goals. Speed in the writing has a tendency to cause a separation, a spreading-out of the *M* and *N*, hence more diagonals are found.

gestion about meme man + also wonder news editor received.

Lower Zone Diagonals

Since the lower zone is associated with physical energy, diagonals found here indicate the energy that supplies the motivation for hard work and physical drive to get the job done. It is also an indication of the writer's desire to achieve.

Personally matter of

Personnel Potpourri

The Friendly Co-Worker

The warmth of friendly staff relations is a good incentive for going to work each morning. The affectionate and considerate co-worker has a right-slanted writing, revealing a responsiveness to others—a willingness to share his sympathies. Soft, rounded garland connections show a compliant approach to life. An "average" size of middle zone letters points out the person who can fit into almost any kind of social situation, official and personal.

uy noon luncheons

Friendly, compliant co-worker

The Generous Employee

The ability to endure and to enjoy the "give" in the "give-and-take" of the working world is found in the generous spacing between lines, words and letters. At times, *t*-bars will cover the whole word which may end with long, upswept appendages. Quick, large writing is another sign seen in the handwriting of a generous soul.

much the 'e way he ray others

Generosity

The Traveler

Some people require a job that keeps them on the move. Never corral the Traveler in an occupational environment where physical activity is lacking.

A large writing with long, full lower loops signifies an active person; one who makes a good salesman, delivery person or outside worker. If you must place such a person temporarily in an office, seat him across the room from the water cooler and down the hall from the copying machine. He'll love the exercise.

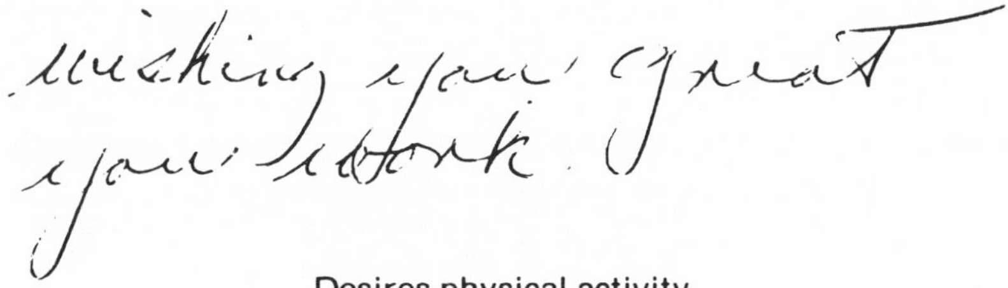

[handwritten text]

Desires physical activity

The Homesteader

There's also that sedentary creature who hates the thought of moving. He likes to plant himself firmly at his desk in the morning and not budge until time to knock off. To find the employee who likes to set up camp at his desk, look for slow, rather small writing with a scant lower zone. If the employee is a man, he may earn the name Barnacle Bill; if a woman, "Wonder-Buns". But they can concentrate on detailed work for long hours while thoroughly enjoying themselves.

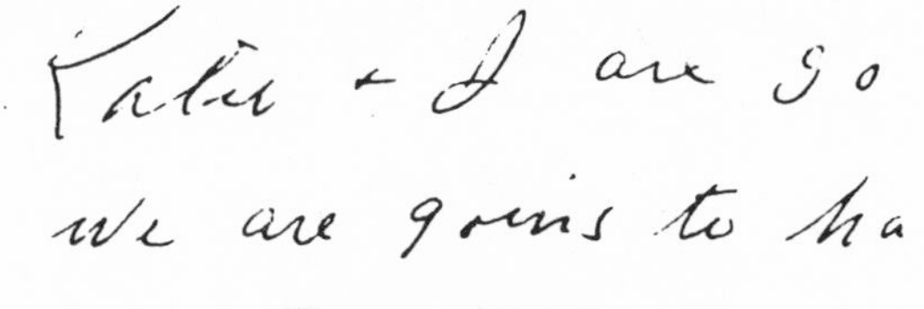

[handwritten text]

The non-athlete

The Diplomat

The tact with which your employee treats his fellow workers and your customers is measured in tapering words in handwriting pleasing to the eye.

If the script is crudely stroked with awkward, unsightly letter formations and an uneven baseline, with tapering words then this exposes evasiveness.

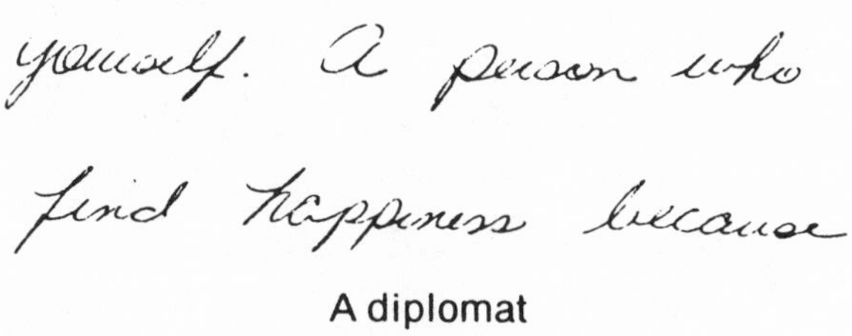

[handwritten text]

A diplomat

63

Conniving evader

The Favor Seeker

One who goes out of his way to ingratiate himself with those in authority by flattery or by service, or even assuming unwarranted blame writes a gracious-looking script in which the *m* and *n* looks like a *w* and *u*. When these cup-like formations are drawn with loops, they can look like a row of *e*'s. The writing becomes hardly readable.

Favor seeker

Avoiding Office Conflicts

Signs of Domination

Domination or bossiness can be found in the vertical down-strokes which end abruptly at the baseline. Most often these letters are the *m*, *n*, or *h*, and occasionally the *t* and *d*. When combined with lower loops that are sharply triangulated and *t*-bars sloping downward, you have a bossy person who is difficult to be around no matter how well he does his job.

Domination

The Quarrelsome Employee

Temper and resentment are bound to create a quarrelsome nature. To evaluate temper, look for tiny strokes known as temper tics found at the beginning of strokes in the upper and middle zones of writing. Resentment shows up in stiff, straight beginning strokes, especially if they begin below the baseline. Impatient slashes for *i*-dots and *t*-bars further identifies the shoulder which has a chip on it.

many thanks

Quarrelsome

Office Jealousy

To expose jealousy, look for these three signs: cramped loops on the capital M, N, and H denoting tension and self-involvement; extreme right slant showing a strong dependency on others, and end strokes which curve back to the left, revealing selfishness. Contrary to popular belief, green eyes are not one of the signs.

Hi! Monday I went out for pizza

Jealous

Stubbornness

Stubbornness carries the act of resistance beyond determination and persistence to where the writer may resist even something he really wants to do, just for the sake of the ego.

The most obvious sign of stubbornness is braced, tent-like strokes of the separated *d* and *t*. It is often found in angular writing, and the heavy pressure which indicates strong emotion-al intensity demanded for this trait is a dead giveaway.

Stubborn

The Busybody

Check how your job candidate forms his capital *H* and *K* to find his degree of personal interest in the office family and his willingness to become a part of it. One who prefers his privacy will not connect the two sides of these letters. He who is involved in the affairs of others will bridge the gap. The busybody, how-ever, will carry the stroke back through the stick in an excessive movement.

Aloof   Involved   Busybody

Arrogance

An overbearing manner which cloaks feelings of inferiority can be detected by extremely tall *t*'s and *d*'s combined with larger-than-average capitals out of proportion to the rest of the script.

66

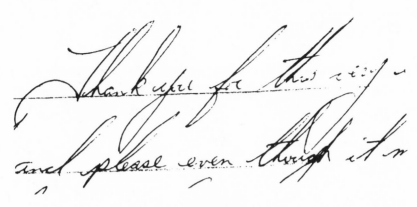

Arrogant

This writer's personal pride and ego is excessive. The points on the upper zone letters indicate he will question any new idea presented to him. If that idea doesn't compute with what he already knows, it's wrong!

The Peacemaker
Every office needs at least one employee who can see the fireworks coming and defuse them. This takes a person alert to what is going on around him, but detached from the conflict. He cares, but understands both sides. And he has the intelligence and awareness to pick the right time to step in.

This script is often a combination of printing and cursive writing. Printed capitals and separated letters that are sprinkled throughout the writing indicate the diplomat who is versatile enough and is knowledgeable about human nature so he can recognize what is going on. His own ego is firm, as shown in the medium to large capitals, and his straight baseline indicates his firm purpose of direction.

Dear Eldene,

Have just returned from England and a pile of mail awaited me. Made copies of the enclosed for you and will keep you informed as more replies are received.

Peacemaker

The occupational personality that fits in with your company will not only make the daily work go more smoothly, but it will also enhance your company's image. This, in turn, creates cash in your till. Decide what writing features and personality traits you want in your company. We recommend that you ask for professional help from a trained graphologist.

Chapter 6
OTHER HIDDEN POTENTIALS AND TALENTS

Although the everyday practicalities of business are fairly routine, many industries need a more creative approach. Every business can use some imagination. The idea man shares this trait with the creative artist. In Dale Carnegie's book, "Managing Through People," he says:

"One of the chief barriers to creative thinking is the tendency of most people to conform to the customs and practices of their environment. They fear being different in their thinking just as they fear being different in the way they dress, talk and act. Usually it takes an iconoclast to come up with the radical new ideas that may really make a significant contribution to solving problems."

Napoleon thought the human race was governed by imagination. Joubert considered imagination "the eye of the soul." Einstein declared imagination more important than knowledge. And imagination can easily be recognized in the handwriting!

The word talent is often thought to mean artistic talent, limited to painting, drawing, dancing, music or writing. But there is a talent for creative thinking which, when applied to industrial problems, creates new methods for old, new directions of thinking which have no boundaries.

Traitmatching Creative Talent

Suppose you needed to hire an interior decorator. The applicant should have imagination and some cultural interests. The job also calls for a love of color, an interest in new ideas, an eye for form and composition. But you also need someone with a good practical sense so that you can live with those ideas.

A page of script can be as pictorial as an etching. The script can be either large or small, but the margins are pronounced and look like a picture frame. Every line flows neatly across the paper and down the page. The beauty of the writing is enhanced by its uniqueness, whether printed, written, or a combination of both.

Creativity is the coupling of originality and imagination. Originality is really the birth of new ideas, imagination the unique use of them.

In Chapter Three we learned that script simplification, writing which departs from the copybook stereotype, is a sign of originality as well as intelligence. When combined with strange or unusual letter forms that are pleasing to the eye, you have found real creative potential.

The nucleus of imagination is full loops blended into the upper and lower zones giving the whole writing appeal.

Because creativity is born out of imagination and originality, the feelings—represented in pressure—which accompany these talents should be strong. A heavy pressured writer is bound to have an appreciation for color.

The writer who combines printing with writing has the versatility to be both practical and creative. If he develops a business around his creative efforts, he is likely to be successful because he can visualize realistically the cause and effect results his ideas will bring.

Artistic writing

70

Talent-Scouting With Handwriting

Manual Dexterity

Flattened *r*'s, *m*'s and *n*'s resembling cogs in a wheel shows the creativity of one who works with his hands, whether painting on canvas, playing the violin, or assembling micro-electronic components.

three children

Manual dexterity

Athletic Talent

The Lover of outdoor sports and physical activity combines good rhythm, a well-developed lower zone and firm pressure. Rhythm can be found in the periodical ebb and flow of the writing stroke. Lower loops have an easy swing, are of the same length and have rounded bottoms. By turning the paper upside-down, you can see a rhythmic pattern to the baseline connections.

Holding paper upside-down reveals rhythm

Showmanship

An artistic plus for actors, salesmen or promotional idea men is a flair for showmanship. Combine the signs of creative talent with larger-than-average writing, embellished capitals and a right slant. This blending of desire for attention and a special liking for people is also found in the envied hostess. She will throw excellent parties.

71

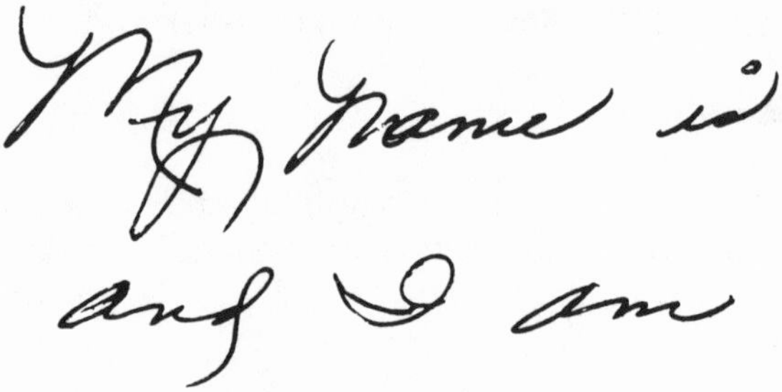

My name is and I am

Showmanship

Aesthetic Training

A quick way to note talent and cultural interests is to look for the shape of certain letters which reflect the writer's creative bent. Refinement shows in a neat, pleasant-to-the-eye type of writing. Greek e, a figure 8 g, a d that curves back to the left in a graceful, rather archaic style and the t that has no cross bar, but uses a right tending curve arching up from the baseline—these are the signs to look for.

All these letters may not be present in every writing, but one or more is bound to reveal the employee who knows how to talk with your more sophisticated and cultured clients.

the

Greek E

going

Figure 8 g

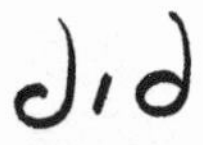

did

archaic d

that

"elegant" t

Circle i-dots

When i-dots are made as a circle, it signals creativity and a need to be noticed. In teenagers, it displays a bid for attention and the beginning of a search for identity. When used consistantly by an adult, the circle i-dot shows a true inner need for artistic expression.

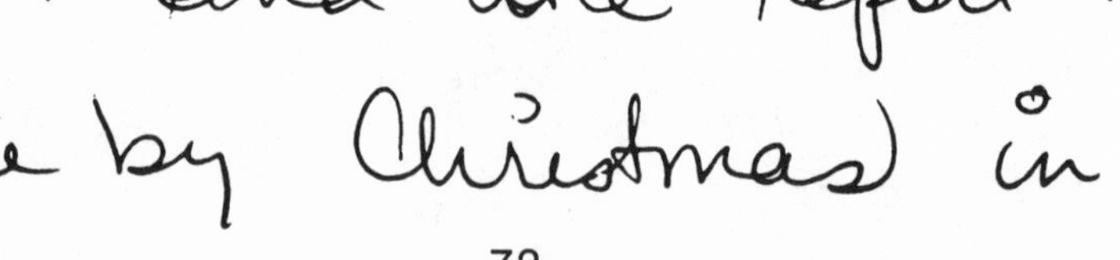

+ send the report ! me by Christmas) in

Dr. Willa Smith, in her report on Creativity for the American Handwriting Analysis Foundation, stated: "Creativity is sensory input manipulated for a meaningful purpose." She went on to note that few research tests have been made on the harmony and balance of writing that equate to creativity, but most people can recognize it when they see it.

"A built-in kernel of creativity is required for the most creative and imaginative people, but some of it can be learned," says Dr. Smith. "Spontaneity, curiosity, flexibility, intuition along with a generous helping of perseverence are all traits found in the creative personality."

This is by far the nicest day of this season, neither too hot or too cold.— it blooms on the apex of perfection — an Edenday Good day for an angels pic nic, They could. lunch on the smell of flowers and new mown hay, drink the moisture of the air, and dance to the hum of bees, Fancy the Soul of Plato astride of a butterfly riding around Menlo Park with a lunch basket Nature is bound to smile somehow, Holzer has a little dog which just came on the veranda, The face of this dog was a dismal as a bust of Dante but the dog wagged its tail continuously— This is evidently the way a dog laughs — I wonder if dogs ever go up to flowers and smell them — I think not— flowers were never intended for dogs and perhaps only incidentally for man, evidently Darwin has it right They make themselves pretty to attract the insect world who are the transportation agents of their pollen, pollen freight via B^(u) Line There is a bumblebees nest somewhere near this veranda, several times one came near me — some little information (acquired experimentally) I obtained when a small boy causes me to lose all delight in watching the navigation of this armed flower burglar.

Here is a sample of Thomas Edison's writing which shows most of these traits.

Talent doesn't always mean artistic expertise. A talent for understanding people or a talent for handling the intricacies of your business is just as important as painting or sculptoring. Be aware that talented thinking can be Traitmatched right along with intellect. Look for the pleasing picture value of a writing as a first step. The fluid and rhythmic movement of the writing across the page is another clue. And if you aren't sure, ask your friendly professional handwriting analyst.

Here is a sample of James Joyce's writing which shows some of these traits.

60 Shelbourne Road

I may be blind I looked for a long time at a head of reddish-brown hair and decided it was not yours. I went home quite dejected. I would like to make an appointment but it might not suit you. I hope you will be kind enough to make one with me — if you have not forgotten me!

James A Joyce

Chapter 7
COMPANY LOYALTIES

Honesty is a beautiful word.

It encompasses many qualities desired in business relationships. Honesty is not an absolute quality, but rather a collection of separate traits. It can mean having the courage and objectivity to tell the truth. Consideration, sincerity and fairness are all found in honesty, as is dedication and reliability. It's also another way to describe integrity and the person you can trust with company funds or materials.

B.W. Overstreet in his book "Understanding Fear," stated that honesty is an absence of fear. The famed psychologist listed courage, loyalty, missionary zeal and ambition as growing out of subconscious fears. But rare is the person who is not afraid of something. Even the "life of the party" has a fear of not being noticed.

Deliberate lying is also rare but fear of disapproval has caused each of us to bend the truth occasionally. You—the very personal You—is involved, and ego plays a strong role shaping honesty. The practical business owner recognizes these subtler frailties of human nature. While he doesn't want a liar or a thief in his business, he does desire an employee who recognizes the virtues of honesty; one who has the maturity and personal moral pride to weigh the circumstances surrounding a situation and make an "honest" decision about how to handle it.

Alfred Adler based his whole doctrine of psychology on the premise, "To compensate is to live; to live is to adjust." Acceptable degrees of honesty seem to abide by this concept of moderation.

The main concerns of an employer are: "Can I believe what my employee tells me? Will this person steal from me? Can I trust this applicant with my business?"

Because honesty is a collection of separate traits, the Trait-match analyst will find a collection of handwriting factors that will, when weighed together, show the potential for honesty—and dishonesty—in any occupational personality.

The Truthful Employee

People don't usually tell deliberate lies, but certain stresses often seem to justify "stretching the truth." It's hard to remain objective when telling the story of "that great golf shot" to an appreciative audience at the 19th hole.

In this day of euphemisms and half-truths, it takes courage to tell it like it is. Will the prospective employee be brave enough to accept the consequences of his frankness, or will he only say what he thinks the boss would like to hear? The secretary who resists telling a blunt statement of fact because "I was afraid I'd ruffle his feathers" can be a serious stumbling block in the progress of the company.

The truthful employee is the individual who can see facts objectively and has the courage to express them.

Objectivity

The objective thinker is discovered by the lack of beginning and finishing strokes (script simplification) and a lower zone resembling sticks. This signifies a simple, direct approach. Vertical tall letters show independence of thought. Exact placement of *i*-dots and *t*-bars shows precision to relate facts, not opinions. The candid person communicates in simple, direct terms. Full ovals of the a's an o's, slightly open at the top, demonstrate frankness of expression. The writer's conviction is evident in firm pressure. More about Objectivity can be found in Chapter 3, "Traitmatching Intelligence."

objectivity

Courage

Courage is reflected in the decisiveness of firm, even *t*-bars. Large capitals signify the ego is strong enough to maintain independence of thought. A measure of full lower loops and some finishing strokes on words indicates the writer's ability to follow through with his actions.

Now is the time for all good men to

Courage

The Trustworthy Employee

Every company yearns for that paragon of incorruptibility, the trustworthy employee—the individual who can be trusted with money, material and time.

The trustworthy employee reveals his stable personality in an even baseline of writing. His healthy ego will be manifested in full, well-formed capitals, firm pressure and a medium or large lower zone. Tall retraced *t*'s display self-pride and his slight right slant indicates his interest in his fellowman. Well formed letters reveal conservatism.

Voc. — Honesty extro version. Only and that, as a think poorly chos

Deception, Lying and Stealing

A deceptive person may be prone to lying (verbal deception), prone to stealing (deception in action), or both. In any case, his main concern is himself, as he attempts to avoid certain pressures, manifested as fears.

77

Fear, after all, is an anxious concern arising from the stresses of living. A person may never actually commit a dishonest act until pressure is applied and the opportunity is presented. Any employee is most likely to be an honest employee if these two pitfalls are avoided.

Potential dishonesty will show up to some degree in all handwriting samples and must be judged against the strength of the honesty factors also present. Anxiety, fear, a poor self-image and vacillation all contribute to dishonesty. *Therefore, to judge dishonesty in handwriting, at least five signs of dishonesty must appear consistently and repeatedly before the writer is labeled dishonest.*

A wavy baseline is one of the first signs to look for. It exposes a moody, restless individual.

It takes control to write a straight line. A writer who has difficulty keeping his letters on the line is a person who finds it hard to control his emotions. In certain positions, such as a speaker, politician or public performer, these traits can be beneficial. The flexibility in the occupational personality as manifested in an uneven baseline could prove valuable here. So it is important to "read" the effect of the baseline into the whole personality.

But it takes a study of the whole handwriting picture to determine whether purpose and integrity are also present. How the writer uses such traits makes the difference between honesty and dishonesty.

Middle-zone letters that suddenly "jump up" within the word (usually an *r* or *s* but it can be any letter) is further evidence of an erratic personality. He may be a wall-flower most of the time but suddenly demands attention at all costs. His behavior can be bizarre or it can be satisfied momentarily by the telling of a rambling story. You can be sure this writer will find some way to grab the immediate attention he craves, and it might be some act of dishonesty in a fit of petulance.

whatever

Concerns me

Jump-up Letters

Deception

A little larceny exists in the souls of everyone, but most of us have the civilized veneer to control it. Every day we use so-called negative traits in a constructive, positive manner.

Oval letters have been found to be helpful in determining types of deceit. Ovals looped on the left side show self-deceit. Looping on the right, however, is extending deceit outwardly toward others. It can be innocent exaggeration, flattery or an embellished fish story. It can be an excellent tool for the salesperson who extols the virtues of his product while understating its faults.

It is when the ovals are looped on both sides and slightly open at the top that the writer will speak with forked tongue. Double-loops, and even triple loops expose deceit that's intentional, often calculated.

If the double-loops can be found along with strong signs of integrity (straight baseline, even pressure, legibility), it can be a positive trait for a silver-tongued lawyer, a convincing debater or good salesman. But double-looped ovals are one of the strongest signs of deceit. So evaluate with care.

Self-deceit   Exaggeration

Intentional deceit

The deceitful applicant will almost surely show a feeling of guilt and a fear of discovery.

All of us have some little corner of our lives we prefer to keep secret. While some people are secretive merely because they like privacy, others actually have something to hide. The dishonest person has more reason than most.

He shows signs of ''covering up'' by narrow, cramped retracing of certain upper zone letters: the *f*, *l*, *h*, *k*, and *b*—strokes which are normally made as loops. Retraces in the stems of the *d* and *t* are not secretive strokes as we were originally taught to write this way in school. The same is true of the letters *u*, *m* and *n*. So these retraced letters should not be regarded as having any special significance when evaluating secretiveness.

so I that maybe you knew someone there in the park who could use them - if not give them to the Good Will , Retraced letters

While illegible script can be inconsideration for those who must read the writing, or merely the result of a hand in a hurry, it should also be evaluated as a possible secretive trait.

If you are hiring teenagers for some job, such as a paper route or delivering circulars, discount the illegibility of their script. It is more likely to be the result of confusion and uneasiness than dishonesty. Strange feelings occur during puberty and teenagers feel a need to be secretive; at least until they have learned how to cope with the unfamiliar new emotions stirring within them. Secretive, yes, but in this case, the writer doesn't know the secret, either.

very important to me. In my many competetive sports and try

Teen writing

Many liars, thieves and confidence men follow their nefarious paths because of their ego needs. Either they want to be stimulated by the "game" or they need to be soothed or avenged. The ego, bruised or inflated, is the motivating factor. Extremes of the capital *I* become obvious. Huge, embellished, fancy *I*'s showcase the show-off preoccupied with his ego. Very small capital *I*'s reveal a poor self-image.

I have always

Big ego

I took in se

Poor self image

Leftward tendencies in the writing can come from a left slant or from ungainly leftward final strokes in any style of writing. Even inflated loops are a leftward tendency since more ink or graphite is expended on the left side of the loop while the right side stays almost the same. All of these leftward movements are further evidence of the writer more involved with self than with others. Light or varied pressure can display unsureness.

Signs of self-involvement

Theft

The Pacific Telephone Company operates on the premise that ninety-nine percent of the people who use their product are honest. Yet elaborate security systems are installed and employees are bonded. Like most companies, PT&T is critically aware that in-company stealing is a tremendous problem.

Surveys of other businesses show personnel managers consider honesty only superficially when hiring, if at all. Until Traitmatch, there has never been a practical way. The job interviewer's highly questionable intuition ("I just had a *feeling* we shouldn't hire him!") is about as close as most companies come.

Stealing runs the gamut from lifting a pencil to embezzlement. Fears come strongly into play in theft; from being "afraid I won't have a pencil to use later so I took this one," to an emotional crisis that prohibits one from thinking clearly, such as the unexpected illness of a loved one sweeping away a life savings.

Greed is perhaps the most frequent, possibly the only truly basic motive for all crime. In theft, greed is usually born out of the self-involved ego and the excessive desire for a material thing or things.

Acquisitiveness is found in tiny initial hooks; those hooks discovered at the beginning strokes of words. The more you find, the stronger the writer's desire for material things. If initial hooks are found in writing which also reveals good business skills, it might have been written not by a thief, but by a successful antique dealer, junk collector or flea-market trader. But when initial hooks are found in combination with the written signs of fear and deceit, the writer is likely to rip you off for much more than you can afford.

Initial hooks

Sometimes there is a "claw-like" appearance to the writing of one grasping for possessions.

Excessive acquisitiveness

Greed and need are not the only reason people steal. When an opportunity for quick gain presents itself and depending on the risk involved, one who is thought to be "honest" may accept the challenge. His motive may be a sense of rebellion or adventure. Looters during a disaster seldom plan in advance a robbery of an unguarded store. Caught up in the adrenalin-saturated environment of a riot, earthquake or flood, even you or I might yield to a spontaneous temptation we would otherwise resist.

How then, do you screen out job applicants who are likely to steal from you? The dilemma which has plagued businesses for years now finds satisfaction thanks to the developing science of graphology: *you reject immediately those applicants whose handwriting exposes at least five signs of fear or deception.*

SIGNS OF FEAR AND DECEIT = Tendency toward theft.
(five or more)
- Uneven baseline
- Middle-zone letters that "jump up"
- Deceitful ovals
- Cramped, narrow retracing
- Illegibility
- Extremes of the capital *I*
- Leftward tendencies
- Light or varied pressure
- Initial hooks or "claws"

The Honest Employee Myth

Making the statement that someone is honest doesn't guarantee their honesty. It's only implied that the person is likely to react honestly in most situations. Evaluating an applicant as dishonest doesn't guarantee his dishonesty, either. To make such a claim would leave you open to a lawsuit for libel. However, if you find five or more signs of fear and deceit *repeatedly* and *consistently* in the writing, you've exposed the individual who is likely to steal if given the opportunity.

It bears repeating that you will find some of these signs in all handwriting samples. If you've made up your mind to hire only "completely honest" people for your office, you'll be sitting there alone for the rest of your life—and if you were "completely honest" with yourself, you wouldn't be there either. What about that clever dodge on the borderline tax loophole? Or instructing your secretary to say that you're in a board meeting and you're at the handball court? Have you attempted to convince your children that there really is a Santa Claus? Can you really be sure how you would act if you found a dollar bill on the sidewalk? What about a $10,000 bill?

In business, it's important to decide just where one is willing to compromise and determine your willingness to adjust to the various degrees of honesty found in the occupational personality.

Dedication

Employees hired for a permanent job are often sought for their staying power as well as for their work skills. Dedication to the company, while found to some extent in the past history and background experience of the applicant, is usually another guessing game for personnel directors, evaluators and interviewers. The Traitmatch analyst, on the other hand, has solid evidence of the applicant's potential for becoming a loyal, dedicated member of the company family.

The dedicated individual will display good balance in all zones. Short final strokes on words and a firm, steady baseline indicates steadfastness. Consistent, carefully formed letters show attention to duty, enhanced by firm pressure and precise *i*-dots. High, carefully placed *t*-bars reveal pride in self.

specific details

The Secret Keeper

How will you check for the applicant who will keep your company's secrets? If you thought about evaluating for traits of dedication combined with the characteristic of secretiveness, revealed in retraced loops, you've begun to grasp the essence of the technique of Traitmatch! Also look for neatly closed *a*'s and *o*'s.

Dear Eldene —

Just a quick note

Loyal secret keeper

Some Company Handicaps

Vanity

The company blowhard is spotlighted by large, elaborate, embellished capitals:

Happy New Year

Time Waster

Excessive beginnings and finals, plus large writing will cue you to a potential thumb-twiddler. While this person may hide the fact that he wastes time, his supervisor will soon recognize that he takes ten minutes to settle down to work in the morning (beginning flourishes) and may spend more time than is necessary finishing up a job for fear of being wrong somewhere (long ending strokes). He is much too generous with your company time. If these strokes are straight and stiff, beware; he harbors resentments.

a great day

Material Waster

Excessive strokage in the lower zone reveals a poor concept of the value of company property and its proper usage. Uneven pressure shows impulsiveness of action. Put them together and what have you got? Spaces quickly formed on your stock room shelves.

gang's of

The Gossip

Open ovals show the open-mouthed, talkative soul. Beginning and final strokes that roll inward shows the person with poor taste. I-dots having the appearance of being jabbed on the page expose criticism and sarcasm.

don't tell him

Honesty is often a contented state of mind. If things are going well, most of us are happy in the job. We receive normal appreciation for our work, so there's no real incentive to be dishonest (even though the writing indicates some weakness in this area). But if an employee is suffering financial problems, he is more apt to help himself to the petty cash. If his job makes embezzling easy and he succumbs to temptation, the employee may be only half at fault. The boss can protect himself and the company with a periodic *Traitmatch*, thus anticipating the stresses of his employees and removing temptation.

A young mother who worked for a department store had five youngsters of school age to support. For nearly six months she seemed pleased with herself and her job and her supervisor commented to the employer on her good work, especially with difficult customers. Then as the hot summer months blended into autumm, the supervisor began to suspect the young mother was not paying for the school clothes she was taking home almost daily. Closer investigation proved the supervisor right and the young woman had to be terminated. The additional tragedy was that the eldest teen daughter, also working for the store, had to be terminated as well.

This was a case of a normally honest woman being caught in a financial bind that had a time element, the starting of school. Any other time she probably would not have succumbed to stealing. But necessity pushed her beyond her capacity for maintaining her level of honesty. This happens. The wise employer prevents temptation by supervising employee purchases and removal of merchandise.

Chapter 8
DOLLARS AND SENSE

If your new employee will be handling company funds, inventories, invoice numbers or telephone indexes, determine his potential number sense. Does he have a realistic comprehension for figures? An adeptness for structural combinations essential for bookkeepers, tellers, credit managers, and cashiers?

Look at the application form. Dates, addresses, telephone numbers are all routine fill-ins. Are the numbers well-formed, large enough to fit nicely in the space provided? It's an indication the applicant is adroit with mechanical things, including money. If the figures are drawn and spaced in a sloppy manner, your candidate has a somewhat sloppy attitude about himself and his life at the moment. It may well affect his work as soon as he is familiar with the routine.

By The Numbers

When a job applicant has a good vocabulary and a natural ease with language, we say he has a way with words. Likewise, when someone has good facility with numbers we say he has a way with money. In some occupations, numbers speak as loud as words.

Numbers of average size, performed with reasonable speed show the person who can handle the routine mathematics of daily living. Like words, figures come in groups too, so baseline, spacing, and uniformity of number size reveal the same graphological traits.

Illinois
61108

Routine money skills

Numbers which appear a little larger than the letters that surround them reveals the person to whom numbers, money and mathematics holds more than a passing interest.

I have always been interest.
cs" does hold some relevancy
, if this $2 analysis will
so asking your recommenda.
writing. Preferably some lo.

Financial concern

Sloppy figures indicate a careless attitude with money. A good sense of values has not been developed.

1/13/ 1991

Poor money skills

Precise numbers show a real love for digits. Accuracy for the love of accuracy is apt to be this writer's motto.

FROM (Date)	TO (Date)	Wages Earned	Why did you leave?
9-68	8-71	$768 mo	moved
9-'71	11-74	$800 mo	better offer
12-74	3-76	$1060 mo	

Precision worker

As in writing, seldom do we continue to draw numbers the way we were taught. Writers will adopt and use certain formations because it suits their psyche. What may seem strange figures to some can be perfectly comfortable to others.

Archaic numbers, for instance, points to a conservative nature—a clinging to the past. However, people trained in commercial lettering will occasionally use this style.

A writer exposed to mass communication or space-age nomenclature in the past may pick up routine use of the metric 7 or slashed 0. While still somewhat rare to the American public outside of scientific circles, certain occupations, such as radio operators, technicians in the computer business, and some medical personnel use them with comfortable familiarity.

These signs can also become part of the writing of those who desire attention or have a yen to be different from the crowd.

Metric 7   Slashed 0

The figure 9 drawn from the bottom, swinging upward and then circling left is not often seen. It is a weak movement. If interpreted in its broadest, most constructive form, you might find the writer idealistic. But it is commonly a sign of wishy-washy action.

Figures made in such a way that their value is extremely difficult or impossible to determine signals a kind of deception; an inner urge to change or hide what one really means—a warning of dishonest tendencies.

A 4 that could be 11

7 disguised as a 9

A 3 or an 8?

A 5 or a 2?

Letter formations can appear as numbers—a phenomena which occurs in the writing of an eccentric personality with great financial concerns.

Look at the handwriting of billionaire Howard Hughes which contains every numerical digit formation. See Page 91.

Thrift

Major among the indicators of good money sense is the quality of thrift. Conservation of material possessions and planning wisely for the future are just as important as the non-spending syndrome that means thrift for most people.

The care with which a person handles money whether it is his own or someone else's is found in a combination of handwriting signs. Precise *i*-dots and *t*-bars reflect the attention he gives each transaction. Conserving as well as spending to advantage is indicated by short or absent final strokes. Complete and practical use of all materials (including the paper on which he writes) shows up in narrow margins.

A thrifty applicant

been some uncertainty,
as to where I stand, and
I want this cleared up
at once.

4

I do not support Maheu
or Stooper in their
defiance of the Hughes Tool
Company Board of Directors,
and I deeply desire all
concerned to be fully
aware of this immediately.

2

7

I ask you to do every-
thing in your power to
put an end to these prob-
lems, and further I ask
you to obtain immediately
a full accounting of any

9
6

Note: Handwriting has been reduced 64%.

1

and all funds and/or
property to which Mr.
Maheu may have had
access.

As I have said, this
matter has caused me
the very gravest concern,
and is damaging my
company and all the loyal
men and women associated
with me in the very
deepest and far-reaching
way.

3

5

My sincere regards,
Howard R. Hughes

8

91

The Tightwad

In addition to the signs listed above, the penny pincher will squeeze his words together as tightly as he squeezes his money.

Excessive thrift

Generosity

Generosity of money, time and self is revealed in a loose, easy, spacious, rightward flow. Humanitarian gestures are made by those who add sweeping, upturned final strokes.

Excessive expansion with flourishes found in final strokes, *t*-bars and capitals reveals a real spendthrift. Because others can easily take advantage of this writer's exorbitant giving this is another good example of a positive quality turned negative when taken to extremes.

Big spender / patsy

Generosity

The Lower Zone Helps

Graphologists all over the world scrutinize the lower zone of writing when evaluating money sense. The lower zone, according to the German philosopher Ludwig Klages, represents the physical and material aspects of human nature. So compare the lower loops of the *f, g, y, p* and *z* to the other money signs.

Lower zone letters that are simple, perhaps stick-like, indicate a no-nonsense attitude toward material things. Tastes are simple, needs, uncomplicated. The longer and fatter the loops, the more preoccupied is the writer with the things money can buy. Sometimes they resemble Santa's bag full of goodies.

you the money.

Thank you very much !

∧

Simple money needs

reading.

meing knitting.

Loves the things money buys

Other Money Signs

1. Look carefully at the general picture of the writing. Is it pleasing to the eye? While no guarantee that the writer has good money sense, the chances are better if it is clear, legible and reasonably consistent in size, slant, pressure. Check out the person's self-image from the signature and capital I to find the writer who will not be shaken by a close proximity to money.
2. Watch out for lines that tangle each other extensively. There's confusion here which may effect the writer's ability for handling money or anything else in any efficient manner.

Confusion

3. Be alert to the writer's control. The more flourishes, the less control.

Flourishes

4. Angles routinely used indicates a sharp thinker with probing mental ability. The more angular the writing, the more acute and clever the writer is apt to be in money affairs.

Angular writing

5. Remember acquisitive hooks—those tiny, initial hooks found in the beginning strokes of words? While the writer who uses them may collect things other than money; stamps, antiques, cars, shoes, heavy use of this sign is a danger signal. Don't

forget to traitmatch for these, as well as other honesty/
dishonesty traits discussed in Chapter 7, Company Loyalties.
By evaluating the results, you can distinguish between the
prospective employee who will take care of your money and
one who will just take it.

A final word of warning! Don't be misled by lovely-looking writing. The following writing sample was made by a convicted forger
as his petition to the parole board.

> *I feel that I am best suited for work involving the keeping of records, such as would be found in shipping and receiving, inventory control, and supply stock rooms.*

This is "persona writing," a mask the writer uses to cover his
real character. Notice that it looks very much like the Palmer
style we were taught in grade school. The careful "drawing" of
each letter indicates a deliberation, an intentional design to convey something other than the true character. As a forger, this
man had perfected the technique.

Dear George

Handwriting Sample   6-77

Thanks for your thoughts the other evening. As usual I found them to be quite helpful.

The coffee shop I mentioned to you in Mira Mesa mall is literally up for grabs at this point. The present owners are asking $143,000 of which ~~?~~ approximately $60,000 is a note for fixtures and equipment. I have enclosed their ~~?~~ 2 latest statements (the balance sheet I am told is only updated annually). ~~?~~ You can judge for yourself where costs can be pulled out, but it seems that 5 % more can go to the bottom line than now does. The current owners don't have time to watch this store as it is ~~physically~~ geographically separated from their other interests.

The mall location is very favorable in that ~~?~~ it is the largest center in Mira Mesa. Currently a large bowling alley is due to open for business ~~?~~ shortly in the center and a 4 screen movie theater will open by X mas.

I have saved the nicest part for last; The owners will carry paper, if necessary, so put on your thinking cap ~~?~~ + come on down + make an offer.

M·33·RH

Although this is a reduced copy, the unharmonious picture value reveals a writer you don't want to hire.

Sharp angles make him difficult to get along with. Uneven MZH shows inconsistency. Crossouts and tied ovals indicate unclear thinking in spite of his relatively well spaced words and lines.

Chapter 9
HEIROGLYPHICS OF HEALTH

Health problems, whether physical or mental in origin signal their presence through the chemistry of the human system which ultimately affects the brain. The brain in turn coordinates nerves, muscles and bones to guide a tiny trail of ink on paper. Is it any wonder then that handwriting can present a graphic diagnostic picture to the trained eye as surely as the brain wave print-outs of an electroencephalograph?

The medical use of graphology is not new. In the sixth century, the Emperor Justinian remarked in his memoirs that he noticed changes in writing brought about by illness and old age. More recently, handwriting has been studied at many hospitals and institutions including Johns Hopkins Medical School and the Preventive Medicine Institute. Research has been conducted regarding specific diseases such as that done by Dr. Wladimir Eliasberg (Tuberculosis) and Alfred Kanfer (Cancer).

The psychologist, Dr. W. Wolff, known for his use of handwriting analysis in medical diagnosis, says that writing movements are like gestures and they ''express the way you feel. Anything that moves you, disturbs you or excites you—either emotionally or physically—shows up in the marks you make with your pen.''

Another psychologist, Dr. Michael Pace, uses graphology with special laboratory techniques, a microscope and spectrophotometry to determine whether a job applicant uses drugs or alcohol, often being able to determine what kind of drug is used.

While it would be unwise, even foolhardy for you to try to diagnose physical or mental illnesses from the handwriting of job applicants, you can be alerted by the general health pattern pictured in the writing, screen out risks and thus lower the odds of hiring health problems.

One out of every twenty applicants will be a problem drinker. Alcoholism costs American industry 15 billion dollars a year.

While alcohol control programs have met with some success (Illinois Bell Telephone Company boasts savings as much as $459,000 over a five year period), only sixty out of four hundred of the largest companies have active programs. Generally, smaller businesses can't afford to staff and fund such a program, and nobody wants to hire an employee who is unfit for continuous, functional work.

Usually the first indication of alcoholism—poor work performance—is detected after the applicant is hired. Before these costly work patterns develop, the personnel manager using Traitmatch to evaluate applicants can spot unwanted traits which signal imminent danger for the company.

Traitmatch was never intended to be an extensive course on graphotherapeutics, however. So you won't be able to ascertain whether the unhealthy reliances revealed in the handwriting springs from use of alcohol, drugs, complaints of imagined ills (hypochondria), an abnormal need for spousal support or other mental props.

Signs of poor health are sometimes similar to signs of dishonesty in writing. When you think about it, this isn't surprising. Lack of emotional or physical strength caused by illness often leads to "taking the easiest way out." Judgment is impaired. Hysteria and depression may not always be present, but the inevitable stresses in any company increase the risk.

In the hiring process, it's not necessary for you to determine if the applicant is an honest drunk or a thief who won't touch a drop. You don't want to hire him anyway.

Physical illness, poor mental states and emotional shoulder-leaning can cause extreme deviations in any of the basic factors of graphology: slant, spacing, pressure, speed and clarity. You've already become familiar with the major signs which signal ill health—an uneven baseline, fluctuating pressure and leftward tendencies—discussed in previous chapters.

The Healthy Applicant:

Trait	Matching Sign
Control	Even baseline
Physical vigor	Firm, steady pressure
Ability to cope	Consistant pressure

The Unhealthy Applicant:

Trait	Matching Sign
Lack of restraint	Uneven baseline
Weakness	Weak or fluctuating pressure
Erratic and unreliable	Leftward tendencies

Other Baseline Variations

Baseline Sag
The baseline that drops in the middle like a line heavy with laundry signifies one who attains his goals in spite of physical fatigue or depression.

chairmen. I'm particularly concerne about those committees which take so much time — such as the news.

Baseline Lift
This writer has a short energy cycle. He starts with a burst of energy but quickly fizzles out. He can only maintain optimism for short periods, then fatigue and depression take over again. Should you hire him? If you feel like gambling, flip a coin.

The mistake has been

Baseline Stairsteps
Words which slant upwards along a line of writing shows an attempt to control undue optimism. Words resembling a downward stairstep indicates an attempt to control undue pessimism.

wish 10² for Part I. Thanks

Control of optimism

[handwriting sample]

Control of pessimism

Fluctuating Pressure

The human personality strives to maintain a sense of well being with a balance of coherent interaction between body, mind and emotion. When that balance is disturbed—for any reason—the handwriting will reflect the disturbance in a fluctuation of pressure.

[handwriting sample]

Good health: Even baseline with firm steady pressure

[handwriting sample]

Poor health: Uneven baseline with fluctuating pressure

Leftward Tendencies

Leftward tendencies may be found in long, stiff beginning strokes, in final strokes which finish toward the left, in t-bars that don't make it through the stem, inflated loops, and an extreme left-slanted writing.

The writer of a slight left slant may be the perfect employee in a job, especially one in which he works alone, and confirms his good health in an even baseline, firm pressure and constancy of supporting traits.

Interestingly, people who tend to become alcoholics usually have an extreme *right* slant, showing dependency on something other than themselves, but the writing can still manifest many leftward tendencies.

Here is the handwriting of an alcoholic who finally killed himself in a car accident after a heavy drinking bout. Notice the left t-bar, the stiff beginning stroke in "toward," and the excessive leftward loop on the *d*.

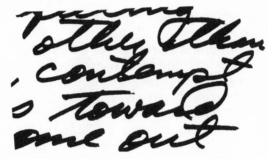

Other Health Signs

Saw-Teeth Script

Alcohol, drugs, old age and nervous problems cause a raggedness of the stroke. If this saw-teeth script is found along with an uneven baseline, it is more likely the writing of an alcohol or drug user. This sample has an even baseline; made by a woman with a nervous disorder.

Saw-teeth script

Heavy Punctuation

Heavy emphasis on punctuation reveals extreme discontent, possibly bordering on hysteria, as in the sample below:

The occupational personality is forever being pushed, prodded and tugged by forces which interfere with his physical, mental and emotional control. Often the pressure will reflect this. David Battan in "Handwriting Analysis, a Guide to Personality" says: Pressure represents a release of energy demonstrating active personality characteristics as opposed to passive, indicating a writer whose ego is healthy and well defined." Sometimes these negative forces are self inflicted as in the case with the alcohol or drug user. In other instances, they may be the result of disease or fatigue. They may be temporary or permanent. Keep these points in mind as you examine the hieroglyphics of health.

Remember that hiring the right person is the name of the game. Look for your applicant's high cards in all of the handwriting areas. See what he has to back them up. What are his overall strengths, weaknesses? Evaluate. If your hand looks good, stand pat. Chances are you have a winner.

Additionally, face-to-face confrontation with a job applicant in a wheelchair or using a cane can present a false picture to the personnel officer. Many physically disabled persons adjust so well in mind, body and spirit, negative health signs will be absent from their writing or compensated for by other highly developed characteristics. Another hiring prejudice is eliminated and the Traitmatch analyst can, by comparing the handwriting of people he has never seen before, find out where the real wounds lie, at the same time increasing his chances for hiring a truly healthy individual.

Chapter 10
THE SQUARE CRYSTAL BALL

I. JOB APPLICANT EVALUATION

In the past, hiring a new employee was a little like searching in a crystal ball. Today, instead of attempting to second-guess fate, you can look into the square boxes of the job application form and predict with reasonable accuracy how the job seeker will act as an employee. Graphological evaluation can be applied to other business forms as well. Credit applications, warranty cards and rental applications to name a few. All provide spaces to be filled in by the user. Rarely is the message crystal clear, but by using Traitmatch, these filled-in boxes can reveal much more about the individual then meets the untrained eye.

Printing

Even the personnel director who knows nothing about graphology automatically scans a job application for legibility and neatness, and judges the job candidate accordingly. But the Traitmatch analyst realizes not all job applicants are comfortable with the "PRINT-DON'T WRITE" instruction often demanded on application forms. Additionally, he can identify persons unfamiliar with printing and recognizes personality variations peculiar to both printers and cursive writers.

Printscript and block printing are the two types of printing commonly seen today. Printscript is taught to children as a primary step in learning how to read and write. The letters have upper and lower zone extensions. Block printing, popular with engineers, draftsmen and commercial artists has only one zone.

good writing ?

High School	PASCHAL HIGH SCHOOL FT. WORTH, TEXAS

Block printing

Applicants who are not familiar with printing often combine printscript and block printing creating a rather clumsy appearance. Take a glance at the signature, too. If the printing is awkward but the signature appears coherent and connected, chances are the writer is unfamiliar with printing. Before proceeding any further, get a good sample of his natural handwriting style on which to base your analysis.

ADDRESS	BUSINESS	YEARS ACQUAIN
55 SANBORNE	Crest House	3
20 Palm, LACANADA	Box Boy	4
33 Vista Bonista LA CANADA	CHecker	4

Signature of Applicant _____ *John Carroline*

' inform

Applicant unfamiliar with printing

During the past century the use of printing as a medium of mass communication has expanded rapidly through the use of machines. Newsprint, typewriting and computer read-outs

104

transfer most of the information in the business world today. Generally speaking, the occupational personality who habitually prints out his thoughts operates much like a machine. He is analytical and objective. He can accomplish his goals with little emotional involvement.

Obviously the printer must use more strokes to form letters. It takes time and concentration to lift the pen and put it down again. Doesn't this indicate that printers will reason with more deliberation and are apt to deal well with small details? He also tends to be mechanical-minded. The cursive writer, on the other hand, is more people-oriented and generally looks at the larger picture in the scheme of things. The habitual printer will use strokes that are fairly even and legible. After all, clarity is the reason why many people prefer to print.

entertainment hoping to eu

interest in Handwriting On

checked were apparent ir

Habitual printer

Some individuals reveal their versatility by using both printing and cursive script with relative ease. They will print for simple readability, switching to cursive writing to express their inner feelings. One young data processor prints all of his memos at work, then goes home and writes lovely poems to his girl friend in a crisp, cursive script.

Here is the handwriting of Thomas Edison, the inventor. He built monumental achievements from precise details. His search for a suitable filament for the electric bulb, for instance, took over four years. His writing style, a combination of printing and cursive script, shows his infinite patience in the intricacies of the letter forms. Note the artistic appearance of the writing. Edison often said that most of his work was "ninety percent perspiration," but it is evident that ten percent of inspiration was also used exceedingly well.

This is by far the nicest day of this season too cold.— it blooms on the apex of perfe Good day for an angels picnic, They con of flowers and new mown hay, drink the m and dance to the hum of bees,   Fancy I astride of a butterfly, riding around Menlo f basket   Nature is boun. Holzer has a little dog which just came on face of this dog was a dismal as a buest of I wagged its tail continuously — This is eviden laughs —

Edison's handwriting—Original, economical

You've heard people say, "I can print faster than I can write," and some printers can be very speedy indeed. Like fast writing, fast printing shows an alert, rapid thinker.

The difference between fast printing and deliberate, methodical printing can be detected in airstrokes. Airstrokes are a discontinuation of ink with a continuation of motion. They are recognized by a feathered appearance on beginning and final strokes of letters. This effect is produced by a quick wispy stroke of the pen. Sometimes airstrokes tend to create a messy look, but it signifies the printer's ability to coordinate thought and action quickly and is a positive sign. So messy-looking printing which contains many airstrokes reveals executive potential, the natural outcome of rapid-fire decision making.

You can traitmatch for intelligence too, since script simplification can be found in printing. The letter *k* is a good example. If it is made with only two strokes rather than the three strokes ordinarily used, the writer has found one of many ways to simplify his script, thereby making it easier and faster to communicate his thoughts. In legible script, it is a sign of intellectual maturity.

Will Call Me

Occidental College

GE

Air-strokes

Slow, unreadable printing lacking air strokes should be evaluated the same as illegible cursive writing. The writer has neither the time nor inclination to communicate. A job applicant could be double-parked, anxious to proceed with the hiring process, or attempting to hide behind unreadable vagueness.

Illegible printing

107

The X-Rated Applicant

Many boxes on the Square Crystal Ball are arranged so they can easily be filled in by the applicant with the letter x. The manner in which the two strokes are made can be significant to the Traitmatch analyst.

The letter x registers your vote. It can become a kiss, and can still substitute for a signature. It's half of the game of tic-tac-toe and even tells you something about movies. No other letter of the alphabet is as versatile as the letter x. But most important to you, the x is also found on many forms used in the business world. The way it is made can give you a peek at the basic personality of the mark-maker.

Take a look at your own x. Are you reserved? Chances are you make a narrow x. the narrower the letter, the more timid or inhibited you are.

If the x is sprawled broadly from left to right, you really enjoy life, giving much time and energy to discovering new friends, new enterprises, new experiences.

Reserved   Enjoys life

Seldom are x's symmetrical. If the point on the upper left is higher, you are a diplomat; one who can survey the situation and tactfully say the right thing at the right time.

The x which is longer on the upper right stroke shows a writer who is aspiring to acquire more knowledge, has many ideals, and works better with theory than with material things.

If the lower right leg of the x is the shortest, it is indicative of a social climber or the ambitious business man who drives himself to betterment.

The short left leg shows a writer who will step down to let someone else take over.

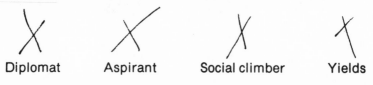

Diplomat   Aspirant   Social climber   Yields

Remember that any single letter merely hints at the occupational personality. It is only a tip of the iceberg. If your company does not yet have a written sample included in the job application, stress the need for at least two pages of handwritten material that should be requested from the applicant. Further, instructions at the beginning of the job application should be changed to read, "WRITE OR PRINT IN YOUR NATURAL HANDWRITING."

The Signature

Throughout your lifetime, no other combination of letters is more refined and polished, rehearsed and revised, tinkered and toyed with, than your own signature. We instantly recognize friends, relatives and business associates by signatures, even if it be an illegible scrawl. Banks still require most transactions to be signed. The personal signature is the supreme identifier and deal-clincher. Since the written name is so important to its author, it holds special graphological significance, and provides very useful information not otherwise available.

The Given Name and The Family Name
If your applicant's given name is larger than his family name and is made with a larger capital and possibly flourishes, it shows a pride and self-identity. If these signs are excessive, they indicate narcissism or conceit.

Signature _____

Pride in self

SIGNATURE OF APPLICANT

Conceit

Emphasis on the family name indicates strong family ties:

Signature

Strong family ties

Social changes can affect the signature, too. It has been observed that women, recently divorced or contemplating divorce, tend to disparage their assumed marital name. Happy brides, on the other hand, display their new marital status with pride—like hanging a trophy on the wall after the hunt.

Newlywed   Divorced

The way in which your name is written by someone else is an indication of the writer's interest and respect in you. As a general rule of thumb, the larger the capitals used when your name is written, the more important you are in the life of the writer. Discount the salutation of letters, almost always written larger than average to attract the attention of the reader.

When writing letters to her father who was constantly away on business, one teenager unconsciously never capitalized "dad", but never failed to capitalize other people involved in her life. The father's long absences had made him seem vague and unimportant to her. Upon his return, however, the capitalization of his title would reappear.

Underscoring

Since underscoring obviously demonstrates an emphasis to the signature, it shows a desire to emphasize, to draw attention to one's self. Huntington Hartford calls underscoring "perhaps the surest sign of the ego." The writer is saying to the world, "Look at me!" Whether it is a sign of self-assurance or conceit remains a mystery until exposed by further analysis of the script.

Underscoring

While some information can be given by the signature alone, you will need a full written page or two in order to make sound graphological judgments. It cannot be over-emphasized that only when certain combinations of graphological signs appear repeatedly and consistently in the handwriting can you then conclude the personality trait they represent actually exists within the individual.

Comparisons of the signature to the body of the script helps to identify compensating, deviating, and covering up of the true personality. If a person's signature is the same as the body of script, he wants the world to witness the totality of his personality. The following illustration shows the meanings of other differences:

Type of Signature		Body of Script		Evaluation
Large	+	Small	=	If legible, healthy ego and self-confidence. Feels his work stands on its own merit. If illegible, insecure. The individual feels he must draw attention to himself by enlarging himself on paper.
Large	+	Large	=	Demands attention. Elbow room needed.
Small	+	Small	=	Modest and reserved. Concentrates well.
Small	+	Large	=	(Rare.) Shy, retiring. False humility. Self-hate if found with illegible script and small capital I.
Legible	+	Legible	=	Considerate, likes to communicate.
Legible	+	Unreadable	=	(Extremely rare.) Possibly not familiar with language, such as foreign nationality.
Unreadable	+	Unreadable	=	Inconsiderate, illiterate, or too busy.
Unreadable	+	Legible	=	Someone who signs his name often; a desire to hide, or both.

Would You Hire This Man?

This sample of writing contains some printed capitals, but uses cursive writing for the rest of the words. The cursive letters seem to flatten out, a sure sign of the haste in which this memo was written. Here is an example of a quick thinker and one who also implements his ideas quickly.

The muddiness of the ink distribution may be caused partially by the type of pen the writer used, but it also shows, graphologically, that the writer is one who indulges his own desires, and probably puts his own interpretations on events. He will bend his values to expedite an issue just as he "bends" and "threads out" the letter form.

The initials with which the memo is signed and repeated at the recommendation area at the top left of the page are strong, showing the confidence and ego of the writer. But notice that the "signature" intitials are larger than any on the page. He expects his suggestions to be carried out.

The Iran/Contra hearings seemed to confirm the personality of John Poindexter as revealed in this memo. He would be a good person to hire for a management job that requires decisions and self confidence, provided his values and goals were similar to those of your company or that he would have regular supervision. Otherwise it wouldn't be long before this type of person would be injecting his original and sometimes unorthodox methods into your business.

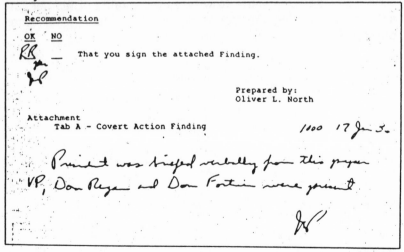

Closing section of Lt. Col. Oliver North's "Memorandum for the President" shows hand-written note, signed "J. P." (for John Poindexter, former national security adviser).

II. CUSTOMER EVALUATION

So far Traitmatch has been shown as an effective employee selection device. But the same graphological signs that define the occupational personality can be used to evaluate customers as well. For example, James McNeal, head of the Department of Marketing at the School of Business at Texas A&M University, suggests studying the handwriting on warranty cards to see what kind of buyer is attracted to a certain product or to a particular store. He points out that advertisements are aimed at specific personality types—another business arena where graphology is useful.

Apartment managers skilled in the use of Traitmatch can evaluate the rental applications of prospective tenants. Insurance firms use it to hire salesmen and to check for health problems in the handwriting of customers.

Salesmen can instantly recognize the need for a friendly approach to the right-slanting customer—or telling the writer with a small, cramped script how much money he'll save—or explaining the working mechanism of the handy-dandy vegetable slicer to the housewife who prints.

Outside of personnel selection, probably the most useful arena of graphology for the businessman is in the screening of credit risks. Henry Durant, director of the Gallup Poll in London, tells of the owner of a mail order house who successfully used handwriting analysis to screen credit applications over twenty-five years ago. Here in the United States, one bank vice-president said:

"A credit manager has an added 'ace in the hole' if he can discern from handwriting that a credit applicant has pride, ethical approach to problems and is orderly and well-balanced. If on the other hand, a specimen of writing showed vanity, excessive generosity or extravagance, ostentation and impulsiveness, the credit manager would do well to think twice before granting an unsecured loan." (From "Value of Handwriting Analysis in Bank Work", Burroughs Clearing House.)

BIRTH DATE (mo/day/yr) 10-3-29	SOCIAL SECURITY NUMBER
Stately *Jane*	007 / 58 / 6013
NAME (LAST) (FIRST)	(MIDDLE)
8765 *Maine* *Street*	

Pride, order, balance

113

medical attention –

Sonia Pope

Vanity, impulsiveness

How to Spot Fraudulent Checks

You've seen how writing is a physical outcome of thinking. It takes coordination between mind and muscle to write, so that when the mind is attempting to produce a false picture, the result will be reflected in the handwriting. Alert your employees who handle checks to look for these caution signs before cashing them.

Hesitations

A person who deliberately pays for merchandise knowing the check won't clear the bank often exposes the deception with hesitations, especially in the round letters *a, o, d, g* and *p*. They can appear anywhere, however. In the sample below, notice the hesitations in the capital *A* and the small *c* in "Alice."

In Southern California, an alert cashier foiled a large, well-organized, quarter-million dollar fraudulent check-cashing ring because she happened to notice that the final upstroke on a signature was a little shaky.

Check for pressure variations and letter patching, which also help to expose the hesitant writer.

Alice Jones

Hesitations

Pay To _____ *Thirty Drugs* _____

_____ *Twelve - 38/00* _____

Patching

Blots and Blurs

Blots and blurs can indicate a guilty conscience. Blobs of ink inside and outside of the letters and smeared places are likely to be nervous reactions from indecision. When it occurs on the front of the check as well as in the endorsement, be suspicious of its validity.

To _____ *Safeway Stores* _____ $ *36 12/=*

Thirty Six and 12/00 _____ Dollars

Difference in Inks

The face value of a check can be altered by adding a "ty" to a check made out for six, seven, eight or nine dollars and placing another zero in the numerical amount. This kind of deception is not common anymore but you never know when it might be tried on you. Look carefully and be sure the ink is the same for the entire check.

To _____ *Alma Smith* _____ $ *80 00*

_____ *Eighty and no/00 Dollars* _____

Raised check

Erasures

An erasure is a clumsy attempt to change a check. We all make mistakes, but a check is not the place to erase. The business person who accepts a check with an erasure deserves the loss.

Ask for another check. An honest person will replace it.

Endorsement and Signature Similarities

Check-cashing employees ask customers for additional identification to verify the signatures were made by the same person. They should also compare the signatures on the front and back of the check to be sure they were not written by the same person. Look for similarities in the more obvious signs like slant and size of the writing and the shape of the letters. Pay particular attention to the capitals, often a dead giveaway. If you have the slightest doubt, ask the individual to repeat the endorsement.

and 93/00 . _____DOLLARS

Tom Easton

3 3860

Signature

Frank Mast

Endorsement

Although an attempt has been made to disguise the writing on the endorsement, notice that the *T* and *F* are shaped the same and there is a break before the *t* in both signatures.

Chapter 11
TRAITMATCH YOURSELF INTO YOUR DREAM JOB!

Are you presently out of work, or hopping from job to frustrating job? Or are you dissatisfied with your present position, hardly able to bear another hour of the daily grind? Still searching for your happy niche in life? Then take a close look at your own handwriting and make your dream job a reality!

It truly takes all kinds of people to make up this big, beautiful world, and even in times of high unemployment so much opportunity is available. It's a shame so many are caged up in an occupation they don't really want. One of the reasons is many people take jobs because they need them to survive, not because they *want* them. It's not long before such a person becomes a corporate zombie, a member of the walking dread. He dreads facing another work day but dreads the thought of being laid off even more.

Some feel stuck behind a desk wishing they were out meeting and mingling with people; others envy the convenient luxury of a sit-down job or the security and seclusion of a tiny office, protected from the extremes of weather. Some yearn to travel. Others are miserable because they can't put down roots.

The mere thought of changing jobs can be a little frightening. Why should that be if you are considering alternatives for your future happiness? For one thing, current job-hunting advice can make your skin crawl. You can find mountains of information on resume preparation, interview preparation, test preparation. Warnings emanate from every corner, "Communicate the proper *image*! Wear only the proper clothes. Act this way... don't act that way. Say only the 'right' things, but say them only in the 'right' way!" One personnel director offered 233 questions for the applicant to practice prior to a hiring interview!

No wonder you may be a little nervous about returning to the hiring hassle where you are expected to play your traditional role and contribute to the deception game of the job interview.

Should you then actively pursue a job which will make your life happier—a thought probably considered dangerous and subversive to your spouse, friends, or casual acquaintances?

Yes! And vigorously! Here are some suggestions which have helped many others and can help you, too.

Be Honest

Now that you understand the inner workings of the hiring hassle, it doesn't mean you must continue to be a party to the deception. By being yourself you can feel more relaxed and confident than ever before. Your honesty will be an asset, a pleasant and conspicuous difference to the interviewer. You won't have to preprogram yourself to fit some graven image. Remember that someone needs the unique combinations of qualities only you possess—that special set of talents, traits, skills, and yes, quirks and defects which exists nowhere else on earth.

Realize your value, your true self-worth. Undiscovered for now, maybe. But priceless nevertheless. When you polish the jewel that is you with the self-esteem which springs from self-knowledge, the glare will cause every employer to sit up and take notice. Remember, if you aren't fully convinced of your abilities, how are you going to convince anyone else?

Traitmatch Yourself

Now get to know yourself through your handwriting, *really* get to know yourself! Your own analysis will not only help you to verify what you already feel is true, it will help you discover other things about yourself you may never have accepted otherwise. Above all, don't be shy. Acknowledge the qualities you find. Accept them as a part of your occupational personality. Humility, especially with a potential life-long career in the balance, is a foolish virtue. Be proud of your talents! Shout about them to the rooftops if you want!

But before you venture boldly out into the job-hunting circuit, be sure your self-portrait is as complete as possible, graphologically speaking. Recognize all aspects of yourself which include your limitations as well. Be sure you're honest with

118

yourself. Don't let the idea scare you. If you find some changes may be a good idea in order to enhance your occupational personality, fine. But you—the you of today—is whom you want to know better. You now have the method within your grasp. It's an ink trail away!

1. Am I a down-to-earth person or do I have a more philosophical nature?

Examine your upper zone extensions and t-bar placement.

some of both maybe be possible that

"Down to earth"   large MZ, open, low *t* bars

Large MZ indicates need for physical and emotional interaction. Openness means you can work with others well. Low *t* bars show your practicality.

arrived with the notebook pages floating around

"Philosophical"   High *t* cross, strong UZ loops

High *t* crosses indicate your more intangible goals. The open UZ loops show your imagination and "idea-oriented" capabilities.

2. Would I be happy in an occupation where I travel constantly, or am I really a homebody who would settle for an occasional weekend in Las Vegas or Miami Beach? Am I better suited to work indoors or outdoors?

Check your writing size, expansion and lower loops.

All mammals wean their

(A matter of breaking ha

"Outdoors"   Large MZH, long, full LZ loops

Large MZH (again) show your need for physical space and action. The developed LZ loops place your interests in tangible things like nature, animals, machines, etc.

fond to talk to you of briefly.
Take care - keep well.

"Indoors"   Small MZ, modest LZ loops

Small MZ indicates the person more interested in mental activities than purely physical or emotional. Modest LZ loops emphasize this more sedentary activity.

3. Am I at my best working with people, or would I work better alone?

Traitmatch your slant and letter size.

ted from high school,
didate for the National
, have worked before

"People oriented"   Cursive, right slant

Cursive writing indicates the "feeling person." The right slant reaches out "from me to thee."

she had a grand time, next time
I am on duty and if she is feeling
well enough we would like to
go on a picknick ? ? would you ~

"Solitary worker" Small writing, upright or left slant
Separated words, lines

Small MZH shows mental abilities. Upright or left slant reveals
the independence to work alone without supervision. The separated words and lines demand solitude and space.

4. Would I be more comfortable in a routine job, or one which
   has the thrill of anticipation, not knowing what to expect
   from day to day?

Check for conventional / original letter formations and size.

into his open grave
saved the President

"Conventional" CB style

Round, cursive writing reveals the conventional person who
prefers to work in conservative, practical work for a good wage.

Anyway, it's a pretty
good advertisement !

"Thrill of anticipation" Original, enthusiastic T s

Original looking writing means an original thinker. Long strong
t bars shows the enthusiasm and drive you will put into your work.

5. Can I achieve my ambitions....

Check diagonals, t-bars and pressure.

to any great degree
to be treated, or

"Ambition" Diagonals, High *t*-bars, strong pressure

Diagonals indicate the drive and direction you want to go. High *t* bars show the ambitious ideas you will add. The strong pressure indicates how much vital energy you are willing to use.

6. ....or am I only fooling myself?

Check your ovals.

very much (my more last year). I don't even told my mother.

"Self deception" left looped ovals

Ovals reflect your thinking clarity. Looping on the left means you may be kidding yourself.

7. What's the use of fooling around? It's straight to the top for me!

Traitmatch your Leaderscript.

America greatest contribution to human society has come not from her weapons or ambitions, but from her ideas.

Adlai E. Stevenson

122

"Leadership"   Large caps, strong pressure, harmonious

Large capitals show your confidence in yourself. Strong pressure enhances the energy and vitality. Harmonious picture indicates your ability to balance thinking and action.

8. What about my money skills?

Examine your numbers, spacing, margins, *i*-dots and *t*-bars.

3969 Idaho St Apt 5
San Diego 92104
July 19 1974

"Money skills"   Good number picture

Clear numbers and a "checker" two (2) show money awareness. Spacing of margins and lines indicate your sense of the right way to do things. Precise placement of *i* dots and *t* bars show accuracy.

9. How's my mechanical ability?

Check for use of printing; size and legibility of writing.

I FIND WRITING IN SCRIPT DIFFICULT AND USUALLY PRINT

"Mechanical"   Printing, size, legibility

Printing shows a mechanical mind more concerned with "things" than with people. Large MZH means you prefer large pieces of machinery like computers or bulldozers. Small MZH indicates interest in small things like watches, parts of machines. Legibility reveals your willingness to do a good job which assures you of success.

10. Am I quick to act or cautious about my decisions?

Traitmatch for speed, pressure, beginning strokes, and length of *t*-bars.

123

*and hull, and spar
she left my side;
bear her load of
place of destination*

"Impulsive"   Speed, *t* cross

Speed is sometimes hard to detect in writing; *i* dots and *t* bars that fall to the right of the stem show quick thinking and acting. If the *t* bar is also long and tapered, the speed is greater.

*Enclosed is a
for the Basic boo
handwriting analy*

"Cautious"   Beginning strokes, short *t* cross

Long beginning strokes indicate caution. If there is also a little glob of ink at the beginning, this hesitation is usually caused by fear. Short *t* crosses also help to "pull back" from impulsive behavior.

11. I've analyzed my handwriting, but still have difficulty believing what I found, even though my best friends agree.

Check for brace-like *t*'s and *d*'s and heavy pressure. (Stubbornness)

*We won't do it that
way.*   ↑   ↑   ↑   ↑   ↑

"Stubbornness"   Braced strokes, heavy pressure, blunt

124

Braced strokes in *t*'s and *d*'s are a sure sign of stubbornness. Pressure adds force. Blunt endings to letters or words reflect a blunt tongue as well.

Get the idea? Delve into your own personality with the blinders of self-bias removed. Since job happiness results from the fullest utilization of your uniqueness, you must discover yourself first. If you have any doubts, seek out a professional handwriting analyst who can use your handwriting for a thorough evaluation of your talents and weaknesses. You alone must make the final decision, so search for what you really want by a further step.

Define Your Dream Job

Next, decide what you want to do. What line of work do you desire? What career do you wish to pursue? You will be spending more time on a job than in any other activity. You could easily say the job *is* your life, or should be. So much energy of mind and body goes into preparing for it, engaging in it, and relaxing from it. It's a shame if the heart's not in it, too. Discovering your own occupational personality *prior* to seeking employment gives you greater opportunity for happiness. Rather than fulfilling some employer's job needs, you'll be bringing about the fulfillment of your own personal desires, accomplishing your own individual goals.

Before you define your dream job, get rid of certain preconceived notions which are pitfalls to your goal. First, forget about—

• What other people want you to be (this includes your spouse, friends, relatives, supervisor or boss);

• What you *think* other people want you to be.

For the moment, also forget all of the old criteria normally used to choose a job. Forget how much the job pays. Your goal is lasting happiness, not a paycheck. If you enjoy what you do, money will not be a primary concern. If you enjoy what you do, you also have much greater chance of success, thereby increasing the possibility of better pay!

Forget the promotional opportunities, the benefits, or prestige. Forget the security the job offers, or where it is located. For the present, don't even consider the requirements necessary to be hired for the job! Now you have a good opportunity to discover how you want to spend the rest of your life.

Concentrate On Your Own Inner Desires

Be free from all of the wrong reasons which motivate most people; free from the influence of others; free from restrictive job qualifications.

Ask yourself: What do I really WANT to do?

Do you have any secret ambitions? Dwell on them. Become deliciously absorbed in your dream. Interested in spending more time with your hobby? Often, people desire to do something they already know a little about. Consider job openings in fields related to your hobby, or maybe being in business for yourself.

Don't be side-tracked by costs. Continue to explore your mind for your real interests. What were the tasks you enjoyed most in previous positions? What jobs did you like best? What were your favorite school subjects? Scholastic interests can be related to many occupations.

If you can't narrow your choices down to a particular job, don't worry. Choose several alternatives for now. As you proceed to traitmatch yourself into your dream job, your job goal will become more clearly defined.

You might find it helpful to look through the Occupational Outlook Handbook (U.S. Department of Labor, Bureau of Labor Statistics, Bulletin 1700). It lists over 800 different occupations; everything from applying the candy coating on medical pills to uranium mining.

Determine the Cost and Your Willingness to Pay

Evaluate your dream job in light of the personality traits found in your handwriting analysis. It would be ideal, of course, if the match was exact. If so, you are probably already occupied in your dream job. It's more likely that there are reasons why they don't match. Everything has a price, and the differences which exist between your dream job and your occupational personality is the price you must be willing to pay to make your dream a reality.

Do you want to be president of a firm? A commendable desire if your handwriting revealed that you thrive on heavy responsibility; enjoy weighty decision-making; constant diplomacy; intense physical and mental exertion, and have an almost obsessive ambition. Otherwise, you are not being completely honest with yourself.

If your family always wanted you to enter the convent, but you've always had a secret yen for belly-dancing, and if your handwriting backs up your hidden ambition with traits like rhythm, artistic talent, showmanship and a strong physical and sensual drive, you'd be better off to put a jewel in your navel than a habit on your head.

Do you find you love the outdoors? Turn in your key to the executive washroom and become a lumberjack—or postman—or football coach, if that's what will make you happy. It's your life. Live it!

This doesn't mean rushing out and quitting the job you have now, unless you can afford it. Use your present job as a survival cushion while you prepare for your dream job. The cost of your dream job may be in time and patience; in more education through evening classes or correspondence courses; in making the appropriate contacts who can help you find the job you seek. You will have a clearer picture of your goals and your ability to achieve them by:

A. Honesty
B. Evaluating your personality through Traitmatch
C. Defining your dream job
D. Determining the cost and your willingness to pay

Remember, there's no one better qualified to make you happy than you. Why spend the only life you'll ever have in a job that doesn't stimulate you and make you eager to start a new day?

Follow your star! But before you hitch your wagon up, take a good look at what's inside it. Most important of all, remember that you'll be happiest in a job which utilizes the full potential of your occupational personality. The uniqueness that is you.

APPENDIX I – TRAITMATCH ANALYSES
Medical Receptionist
Handwriting Analysis requirements from: A-B-C- Medical Clinic

From the writing of: "A"—Female—age 24—left handed
From the writing of: "B"—Female—age 32—right handed

Description of Company: _____

A medical clinic of four general practitioners who cater to middle and upper income clientele. The staff, in addition to the doctors and their respective four nurses, includes a bookkeeper, two receptionists and three laboratory technicians.

Description of position to be filled: Medical Receptionist

Requirements of position

1. Must be able to handle the public in person and on the telephone. Must cope with stressful situations involving patients.

2. Needs mechanical skills to use the typewriter, answering machine and computers.

3. Must be able to collect accounts in person and over the telephone.

4. Must transcribe accurate records both medical and technical lab reports.

5. Must take orders and follow specific procedures consistently and accurately.

6. Must work well in a confined area. Three girls work in an 8' x 17' room.

Special requirement:

7. Must not be easily offended. (One of the doctors is gruff, crude and outspoken.)

Personality traits needed

a. cheerful, outgoing personality
b. tact, patience
c. originality, versatility
d. self esteem

a. manual dexterity

a. honesty
b. accuracy with fingers
c. tact, patience, ingenuity
d. persistence

a. accuracy
b. attention to details
c. memory

a. accuracy
b. organization and control
c. consistency in work habits
d. conventionalism

a. somewhat sedentary attributes
b. control, organization
c. flexibility

a. flexibility
b. earthy, not too sensitive
c. persistence
d. self esteem

BASIC FACTORS ANALYSIS
For the position of: _____
From the writing of: _____ "A"—Female—age 24—left handed _____

Basics of handwriting	Comments
● **PICTURE VALUE**	Good, pleasant to look at
● **SLANT**	
Medium	Friendly, compliant
Rightward	—
● **BASELINE**	
Even	Goal directed
● **MARGINS**	
Fair	Shy, reserved
Left narrow	—
Left-left tending	Can work well behind scenes
Right	
Medium	Some fear and hesitation over the future
Uneven	—
● **SIZE**	
Medium	Self esteem, but with reservations
MZ	
Medium	Good general worker
Even	—
UZ–LZ	
Good	Organized, practical
Balance f's	Capable of abstract thinking
Loops	
Few, full	Some imagination
Most narrow	Good for routine office work
● **SPACE**	
Expansion	
Narrow	Thrifty, can work in confined areas
Between lines	
Good, but some	Usually organized thought processes, but
overlaps	occasional confusion when pressures arise
Word space even	Adaptable, consistent
● **PRESSURE**	
Medium	Medium energy level, conservative
● **SPEED**	
Medium	Conventional, efficient, conservative
● **CLARITY** (legibility)	
Excellent	Good communications

appreciate their bodies. In giving nourishment to their bodies they were giving enrichment to all other experiences of their day to day lives. The talk to the women gave me a renewed and refreshing look into my own life.

The trip to Fife lifted my spirits and gave me a push in the right direction. I knew that ~~working with people in the field of health and~~ ~~medicine was important and worth my energies.~~

Recently I finished a course on Medical Office Management. It provided me with instruction in ~~secretarial and receptionist's duties, as well as giving~~ a thorough understanding of the role and responsibility of public relations and professional attitude. I interned at a doctor's office where I had the opportunity to exercise the material I had learned in class. My efforts to help and meet the needs of the patients were rewarded with friendliness and sincerity.

I know that I may look forward to a happy life with work in the medical arena, and that the positive efforts I put into my work will be returned to me.

A. F.

(August 12, 1950)

Note: Handwriting has been reduced 64%.

130

BASIC FACTORS ANALYSIS

For the position of: _____

From the writing of: _____ "B"—Female—age 32—right handed _____

Basics of handwriting	Comments
● **PICTURE VALUE**	Poor, awkward looking
● **SLANT**	
Strong	Outgoing, friendly
Rightward	
● **BASELINE**	
Uneven	Moody
Downslanted	Depressed, pessimistic
● **MARGINS**	
Good	Fits well into her surroundings—reserved
Left-slightly narrow	
Right-wide	Fear of the future
● **SIZE**	
Medium/large	Strong ego
MZ	
Small, uneven	Restless, inconsistent
UZ-LZ	
UZ medium	Practical
f's unbalanced	Limited organization
Loops	
Full	Good imagination
LZ-long, full	Needs physical action
● **SPACE**	
Expansion	
Uneven	Inconsistent in use of time, space
Between lines	
Good, but some	Poor picture value detracts from organization.
overlaps	Confusion evident in the patching.
Word space even	Strengthens consistency and adaptability
● **PRESSURE**	
Strong	Strong energy level intensity of emtions
● **SPEED**	
Medium strong but	Not consistent in speed of thinking and action
uneven	patterns
● **CLARITY** (legibility)	
Generally good but	Generally good communications when she wants
some poor letter	to communicate.
formations	

7 - 9 - 76   "B" - FEMALE - AGE 3
RIGHT HAND

I am the person best qualified for
the position of Medical Secretary due to
both my educational background and
my experience.

Note: Handwriting has been reduced 64%.

FORMER EMPLOYERS (List Below Last Four Employers, Starting With Last One First)

Date Month and Year	Name and Address of Employer	Salary	Position	Reason for Leaving
from 11 - 75 to 3 - 76	The Divine Memorial New Brighton, PA	12,000	Adm. Assistant	Interim - leaving office in CA
from 6 - 74 to 11 - 75	Office of Mental Retardation Commonwealth of PA	18,000	Coordinator for Title I Projects	Child transp. to facility, etc.
from 6 - 69 to 6 - 74	St. Peter's Child Dev., Inc. Pittsburgh, PA	19,000	Unit Supervisor	Higher Paying Position
from 6 - 73 to 6 - 73	Allegheny County Mental Health Mental Retardation Program, Pittsburgh	14,000		Desire for Client Contact

agency or office which services
medically involved and social
and emotional needs of persons,
I...

...M...

i.e. Due to my Social Work background
I would also be able to relate to
clients effectively and efficiently; actually
your agency NEEDS someone like me.

132

TRAITMATCH ANALYSIS
Handwriting factors required by position of: _____
Medical Receptionist

From the writing of: _____ "A"—Female—age 24—left handed
From the writing of: _____ "B"—Female—age 32—right handed

Trait requirement	Handwriting factor	Strong	Medium	Weak/None
Cheerful	right slant	A B		
	upslant baseline	A		B
Tact	diminishing letters		A B	
	good picture value	A		B
Patience	neat, round writing		A	B
	careful i dots		A B	
Originality	unusual letter forms		A	B
Versatility	varied letter form	B		A
	printed & written caps		A B	
Self Esteem	firm pressure	B		A
	medium to large cap I		A B	
	underline signature			A B
Manual Dexterity	squared r	A		B
	balance of MZ & LZ			A B
Money Sense	well shaped numbers	A B		
	compressed letters	A		B
	full LZ loops	A B		
Ingenuity	*unusual* letter combinations			A B
Persistence	tied f's and t's			A B
Accuracy	careful figures	B	A	
	precise i dots, t bars		A B	
Memory	attention to details	B	A	
	firm pressure	B		A
Common Sense	organized writing	A	B	
	control	A	B	
	flexibility	A	B	
Organization	balanced f's	A	B	
	good margins, spacing	B	A	
	consistent slant/press		A B	
Conventionality	medium MZ	A B		
	consistent letters	A		B

133

TRAITMATCH ANALYSIS (Continued)

Trait requirement	Handwriting factor	Degree of use		
		Strong	Medium	Weak/None
	good pressure	B	A	
	copybook I		A B	
Sedentary	short LZ			A B
(non physical)	narrow loops	A B		
	slow writing		A B	
Flexibility	garland, round writing		A B	
	right slant	A B		
	even baseline	A		B
Not Overly	firm pressure	B	A	
Sensitive*	retraced t's & d's	A		B
	full LZ loops	B	A	
	TOTALS	17 15	17 13	8 14

*a specific request because this candidate must work with a doctor who is often crude and bluntly outspoken.

Evaluation for: ___"A"___
Positive 17 out of 42 factors equals 41 %
Medium 17 out of 42 factors equals 41 %
Weak/None 8 out of 42 factors equals 18 %

Evaluation for: ___"B"___
Positive 15 out of 42 factors equals 36 %
Medium 13 out of 42 factors equals 31 %
Weak/None 14 out of 42 factors equals 33 %

HONESTY EVALUATION

From the writing of: _____"A"—Female—age 24—left handed_____

From the writing of: _____"B"—Female—age 32—right handed_____

Note: At least five dishonest factors must be consistently repeated to judge a writing 'dishonest'.

Honest	Strong	Medium	Medium	Strong	Dishonest
	Degree of honesty				
Even baseline	A			B	Uneven baseline
Firm pressure		A B			Light/varied pressure
Right tendencies	A B				Left tendencies
Legibility	A		B		Illegibility
Free movement		A	B		Cramped, retraced, slow
Short initials		A		B	Initial hooks, claws
Even MZ height	A			B	Uneven MZ— "jump up" letters
Copybook cap I		A		B	Extremes in cap I
Consistency	A			B	Inconsistency
Ovals clear		A B			Ovals embellished
			A	B	Ovals looped on left
			A	B	Ovals looped on right
			—	B	Double looped ovals
	— —	— —	— —	— —	Ovals open at bottom
TOTALS	5 1	5 2	2 3	0 7	
	A B	A B	A B	A B	

Evaluation for "A": ___Good sense of honesty___

Evaluation for "B": ___Risk___

SUMMARY OF OCCUPATIONAL PERSONALITY
From the writing of: <u>"A"—Female—age 24—left handed</u>
Recommendation: <u>Hire</u>

Basic personality: This young lady's writing shows a pleasant, friendly, but somewhat reserved personality. Shy at times, she has the tact and patience to maintain a dignified manner which can be an asset in the type of office and with the clientele she is expected to work with.

Work habits: Organizational abilities are good. She approaches her goals directly and works toward them with common sense and some flexibility. She adapts to her surroundings, but maintains caution and hesitation because of some doubt about her abilities in an unknown situation.

She is good with routine work as long as she doesn't take on too many jobs at once. Generally conservative and conventional, she is cautious about applying new or original ideas except in her personal life. Consistent, tactful and cheerful as a rule, she can relate easily to the public. She is seldom aggressive about anything.

Physical attributes: Neat in her work, and probably in her person, Ms "A"'s stamina may not be very strong. She can, however, work reasonably well in the confined area outlined as required in this job.

A good sense of mechanical things, including numbers, money and machines, she also has the dexterity to work with mechanical tools such as typewriters, calculators, etc.

Honesty: Positive and medium honesty factors are split 50/50 out of ten possible factors. With no strong negatives out of a possible fourteen, and only two medium negatives, she is a safe honesty risk.

Honesty and integrity are strong. A good sense of ethics and high standards of behavior assures her conduct in an office of this type.

Special requirement: Evaluation for "not too sensitive" is only fair. She is generally cultured and gracious. Since she seldom uses crudity or vulgarity, it takes her strong objectivity to overlook such conduct in others.

Her self-image is not strong enough to cause her to lock horns with the outspoken doctor. She is more apt to stay out of his way as much as possible. However she is not so sensitive that a personal attack would cause her to refuse to work with him.

Recommendation: Ms "A" has a good personality for the type of work demanded by this position of medical receptionist. She can follow orders, yet maintain common sense when a personal decision is required.

She can add a gracious personal touch to the front office, handle the telephone and accounts receivable work with dispatch and accuracy.

Because she is conventional and rather conservative, she is not apt to want to move around in the job or demand an advancement, unless her personal life makes a change.

HIRE

Follow-up Report on Ms. A.

A-B-C Medical Clinic hired both Ms. A and Ms. B due to an unexpected personnel shortage. Reflecting our recommendation, Ms. A was made head receptionist in spite of the fact she was several years younger than Ms. B. Ms. A adapted well to the new work and gradually gained confidence in her new responsibilities. Her stamina seemed to improve with the challenge of the job; she didn't need time off and she continued to fulfill her duties well. The outspoken doctor seemed to respect her and restrained himself in her hearing.

As of the last report date, August 1986, she was still employed by A-B-C Medical Clinic.

SUMMARY OF OCCUPATIONAL PERSONALITY
From the writing of: <u>"B"—Female—age 32—right handed</u>
Recommendation: <u>Risk</u>

Basic personality: Ms "B"'s writing shows an outgoing person-ality which at times becomes overpowering in its drive and aggressiveness. While she can adjust to her environment she needs plenty of action room. Her moodiness and tendency toward depression—as shown in this and previous samples—is apt to affect those around her negatively. Her sense of humor is good.

Work Habits: There is little consistency in her attitudes or work habits. A strong ego gives her a fighting spirit which helps her to cope with daily problems, but her aggressiveness may go to extremes at times.

Practical, generally organized, she is changeable in her use of time, energy and space, especially when her emotions become involved.

She needs variable responsibilities. Routine bores her. Confusion may often arise out of her inconsistent methods, and she could neglect details through carelessness, although she is usually quick to see the necessary things that must be done.

Physical attributes: Ms "B"'s writing shows a need for physical movement which may make it difficult for her to work within the close confines of these office requirements. She is good with mechanical things. She also has a good money sense and can handle figures fairly well. She has enough adaptability to cope with the vagaries of machines, but would probably enjoy fixing those that malfunction better than using those that require routine use in the job.

Honesty: Ms "B" is too emotionally ambivalent to be depended upon for absolute honesty of action, speech or thinking. She demands attention from time to time, and if she can't get it through good works, she'll create a negative action to achieve recognition, such as gossip, lying, tale-bearing, etc.

"Self" involvement makes it easy for her to rationalize her behavior. Usually honest with herself, she may develop all kinds of "excuses" for unreliable conduc˙

Special requirement: Ms "B" has much sensitivity in her self image, and criticism of her work or her person is taken hard. Her imagination centers in her own emotional viewpoint.

She could "talk back" to the outspoken doctor and join him in his vulgarity, but she would be quick to take offense at a remark she felt was aimed at herself.

Recommendation: Ms "B"'s writing shows she has emotional ambivalence which would make it difficult for her to do consistent and completely acceptable work for any length of time.

Hurt or threatened, she may retaliate with dishonesty, but she would feel justified from her point of view. She is not objective. Dishonesty factors in her writing exceed recommended standards.

RISK

Follow-up Report on Ms. B.

Ms. B. was hired by A-B-C Medical Clinic in spite of our "risk" evaluation. She was assigned to work under the younger Ms. A, which displeased her. However, she worked for two months before she quit, following an angry confrontation with one of the doctors.

TRAITMATCH ANALYSIS
Executive Placement

Requirements for Analysis of Handwriting for specialized positions in management.

Company: Zenith Hotels Inc.

Date: 6-14-76

From the writing of: Henry C. Ohlmeier

Description of company:

A chain of small hotels in resort areas. Clientel ranges from middle age to senior citizens. This particular hotel needs a manager. Present staff includes manager, two assistants, a bookkeeper, two desk clerks plus two maintenance men and twelve maids.

Hotel has restaurant, golf course and tennis courts concessioned out to other companies. An 84 room occupancy, the hotel premises include a pool, recreation areas which house pool tables and penny arcades, dance floor. A few small shops are locally owned. The manager must act as landlord for the leased concessions.

Description of position of: Hotel Manager

Requirements of position	Personality traits needed
1. Must be able to handle hired personnel as well as the public clintele including celebrities who come to the hotel.	a. decisive b. confident leadership c. cheerful, outgoing d. dignity, tact, patience
2. Must be able to host celebrities, accepting all kinds of personalities. Not easily rebuffed.	a. showmanship b. self esteem
3. Must be able to communicate with all types of people.	a. communication
4. Will probably need to work a 12 to 14 hour day at times.	a. physical stamina
5. Must be able to balance his rather complicated budget.	a. money sense b. organization c. decisive
6. Must have intelligence to understand details of the many jobs beneath his jurisdiction. Personnel hiring and managing, mechanical maintenance, logistics of housekeeping.	a. attention to details b. logic c. concentration, control d. versatility, flexibility
7. Must understand the needs of the parent company and how to relate them to the needs of his own hotel.	a. intelligence b. objectivity c. organization

BASIC FACTORS ANALYSIS
For the position of: Hotel Manager

From the writing of: Male—age 47—right handed

Basics of handwriting	Comments

• PICTURE VALUE
Good, strong — Good personality, pleasant

• SLANT
Medium right — Friendly, compliant but firm

• BASELINE
Even — Goal directed, dependable
Slight upslant — Cheerful, generally optimistic

• MARGINS
Good balance medium width even — Adapts to surroundings. Will participate in what is going on

• SIZE
MZ
   Medium size even — Firm ego
UZ versus LZ
   Good balance in f's — Organized, practical
Tall UZ
   Strong — Abstract thinking
Long LZ
   Medium to long — Physically active
Loops
   Medium UZ — Imagination, open mind
   Full LZ — Physically active

• SPACE
Expansion
   Medium — Can work alone or with others. Makes good use of available space
Between lines
   Consistent, but occasional tangling — Generally clear thinking with occasional conflict of thoughts causing some minor confusion.
Between words
   Even, consistent — Adaptable. Maintains contact with self and with others.

• PRESSURE
Medium to strong — Firm ego, good vitality, stamina

• SPEED
Medium — Calm, efficient, unhurried

• CLARITY (legibility)
Excellent — Clear thinking, ability to communicate

141

TRAITMATCH ANALYSIS
For the position of: Hotel Manager

From the writing of: Male—age 47—right handed

Trait requirement	Handwriting factor	Strong	Medium	Weak/None
Decisive	firm t bars	X		
	good pressure	X		
	straight downstrokes		X	
	follow thru finals	X		
Confident	medium MZ size	X		
	strong capital I	X		
	underlined signature			X
Cheerful	right slant		X	
	upslant baseline		X	
Dignity	tall UZ (especially t)		X	
	simple capitals		X	
Tact	diminishing MZ		X	
	good picture value	X		
Patience	neat, clear writing	X		
	careful i dots	X		
Showmanship	flourished caps		X	
	free movement		X	
Self Esteem	firm pressure	X		
	underlined signature			X
	medium/large cap I		X	
Communications	garland (round) letters		X	
	some open a's and o's			X
	clarity (legibility)	X		
Money Sense	well shaped numbers	X		
	compressed letters		X	
	full LZ loops	X		
Organization	good margin spacing	X		
	balanced f loops	X		
	consistent slant/press	X		
Attention to Details	precise i dots	X		
	careful t crosses		X	
Logic	connected letters/words	X		
	consistent pressure	X		
Concentration	small MZ		X	
	good letter form	X		

142

TRAITMATCH ANALYSIS (Continued)

Trait requirement	Handwriting factor	Degree of use		
		Strong	Medium	Weak/None
Control	even baseline	X		
	connected MZ	X		
Versatility	varied letter forms		X	
	printed & written caps			X
Flexibility	round, clear writing		X	
	right slant		X	
	even baseline	X		
Intelligence	simplified letters		X	
	original formations			X
Objectivity	open ovals			X
	good spacing	X		
	simplicity		X	
	vertical writing			X
TOTALS		23	18	7

Evaluation:

Positive __23__ out of 48 factors equals __48__ %
Medium __18__ out of 48 factors equals __37.5__ %
Weak/None __7__ out of 48 factors equals __14.5__ %

HONESTY EVALUATION
From the writing of: _____Male—age 47—right handed_____

Note: At least five dishonest factors must be consistently repeated to judge a writing dishonest.

Honest	Degree of honesty				Dishonest
	Strong	Medium	Medium	Strong	
Even baseline	X				Uneven baseline
Firm pressure	X				Light/varied pressure
Right tendencies		X			Left tendencies
Legibility	X				Illegibility
Free movement		X			Cramped, retraced
Short initial strokes	X		X		Initial hooks, claws
Even MZ height	X		X		Uneven MZ— "jump up" letters
Conservative Cap I	X				Extremes in Cap I
Consistency	X				Inconsistency
Ovals clear	X				Ovals embellished
					Looped on left
			X		Looped on right
					Double looped ovals
					Ovals open at bottom
TOTALS	8	2	3	0	

Evaluation: Strong sense of honesty
Good risk

Summary of the occupational personality of: _____

Henry C. Ohlmeir, Male—age 47—right handed

Company: Zenith Hotels Inc.

Recommendation: Hire

Basic Personality: Mr. Ohlmeier's writing shows he is a pleasant, rather intense man, but friendly and compliant in his relationships with others. He is willing to socialize, but is very much aware of his responsibility to his job. He goes directly toward his goal with quiet determination keeping his mind on his obligations. His cheerful, usually optimistic outlook makes him liked and respected.

Honesty: His honesty is impeccable. He has a strong sense of responsibility, takes pride in his personal integrity. He wants recognition, preferably financial, for his efforts, but he will usually let his work speak for itself rather than demanding attention.

He has an excellent money sense, recognizing the uses and needs of money and the things money buys. He does not waste nor does he spend frivolously, but when the occasion demands, he can be generous. In a questionable situation he may give himself the benefit of the doubt, but he will justify his decision objectively and back it with factual data. He is a fair man. It would not be surprising if Mr. Ohlmeier takes a personal interest in the bookkeeping of the hotel.

Work Habits: Mr. Ohlmeier has enough imagination to initiate new ideas, but practicality and long range worth will be his criteria when implementing them. He is decisive without being domineering, confident without egotism. Usually patient, thorough and controlled, he can be exacting with his employees and he will allow few excuses for poor work. While he cares about his employees, he will expect as much from them as he does from himself...which is considerable. He is more apt to be respected than loved for he can be direct and outspoken in his communication.

Socially Mr. Ohlmeier can fit in well with all levels of society. Although he is conservative and somewhat conventional in manner he can talk with kings or kooks without losing his dignity. His personality makes a good background for the ego needs of most famous people.

Recommendation: Mr. Ohlmeier is well qualified to take the position of hotel manager, especially of a hotel which caters to the adult citizen of upper middle class clientele. He is conservative, honest and industrious with enough imagination to create a pleasant, relaxed resort atmosphere. He is capable of sincere friendship which can bring many clients back to his hotel year after year. Although he can mix well with dukes or drunks, he will show his preference for the conservative among his regular customers.

His sense of identity within the corporation is objective; he can understand the needs of his employers as well as the employees under his management.If allowed to make his own decisions regarding his hotel, Mr. Ohlmeier can make a valuable addition to Zenith Hotels Inc. staff.

HIRE

Follow-up Report on Mr. Ohlmeir.

Mr. Ohlmeir was hired even before my report reached the manager of the Zenith Hotel chain, as the season was starting and no time could be lost.

Mr. Ohlmeir filled the position for three seasons at this small resort, staying on after the season to oversee repairs and manage the minimal staff. He initiated programs for retired persons that brought them to the resort over weekends and during off-season holidays.

Before the opening of the fourth season, Mr. Ohlmeir was asked to transfer to an upstate hotel, newly purchased and somewhat larger but badly run down. His job was to oversee the renovation of both rooms and restaurant, hire new personnel and build up the clientele. He has been successful in doing this over the past six years. Many of his former clients followed him north to the new resort.

At last contact he was still managing the place and anticipated further expansion.

experience to learn how to adjust to the various personality types.

In addition to accomodating people, it also necessary to manage the maintenance of the forty eight room lodge. This necessi. supervising twelve maids, two maintenance and two receptionists. I did all the bookk for the motel.

Motel facilities had both heating and conditioning systems which, over the seven had to be completely overhauled or replace. Swimming pool and tennis courts were also my jurisdiction. Although we had an adj. restaurant, this facility was leased out, a except for advice on maintenance of their and cooling systems, I had no part in the of that establishment.

I feel, because of the variety of my experiences in these very diversified fields am very competent to fulfill the position Hotel Manager.

Note: Handwriting has been reduced 64%.

Henry C. Ohlmeier

APPLICATION   PLEASE PRINT OR TYPE

BIRTH DATE (mo day yr)
12/22/29

SOCIAL SECURITY NUMBER
272 50 2093

NAME (LAST)
OHLMEIER

(FIRST)
HENRY

(MIDDLE)
CARL

ADDRESS (NUMBER)
2720 QUINCY

ST. (STREET)

(CITY)
OCEANSIDE

(COUNTY)
SAN DIEGO

(STATE)
CA

(ZIP CODE)
92054

BUSINESS PHONE 725-4282   HOME PHONE 722-3463
AREA CODE 714   AREA CODE 714

male - Age 46.
Right h

TRAITMATCH ANALYSIS
Computer Programmer

Handwriting Analysis requirements from Company:
Government contract company

From the writing of: Female, age 42, left handed

Description of company:
A company that handles several million dollars of government contracts a year. Hires staff and yard personnel of approximately 2300employees. Produces machinery and material essential to defense. All employees have high security ratings.

Description of position to be filled:
Data processor and programmer in Stock Division

Requirements of position

1. Must have top security.
2. Needs computer skills.

3. Must work without supervision.
4. Must work 12-14 hour shifts at times.
5. Must detect and correct errors in mathematical data.
6. Must solve problems with data provided.
7. Sedentary work.

Special Requirement

8. Solitary work. (Employee is locked in security section during work hours.)

Personality traits necessary

a. Secretive, loyal
b. Manual dexterity, logic, patience, organization
c. Initiative, organization, consistency
d. Physical stamina
e. Alert, good eyesight, understands mathematics
f. Versatile, initiative, logic, accepts authority
g. Geared for mental work, calm, patient

h. Can work in close quarters, solitary, non-social

BASIC FACTORS ANALYSIS

For the position of: Data Processor and Programmer
From the writing of: Female–age 42–left handed

Basics of handwriting	Comments
● **PICTURE VALUE**	Original, reserved person
Arresting, not easy to scan	
● **SLANT**	
Strong left, consistent	Self sufficient, can work alone, non social
● **BASELINE**	
Even, upslant	Dependable, not easily discouraged
● **MARGINS**	
Wide left margin	Independent
Both margins even	Organized, cultured
	Fits into a structured environment
● **SIZE**	
Medium	Self esteem
MZ consistent	Steady worker
UZ tall, narrow	Pride in her work
	Can search for solutions to problems and give extra effort when necessary
LZ long, narrow	Works on nervous energy
Slightly unbalanced F	Better at mental work than physical activity
● **SPACE**	
Narrow letters	A private person
	Can work in confined areas
Wide space between words	Works well without supervision, prefers to work alone
Consistent space between lines	Organized
	Consistent work effort
● **PRESSURE**	
Light to medium	Inconsistent energy level
Heavy downstrokes	Determination
● **SPEED**	
Normal, medium	Efficient, unhurried
● **CLARITY** (Legibility)	
Legible, but not easily scanned	Maintains confidentiality
	Keeps personal affairs private
	Can give clear information when dealing with impersonal data

149

TRAITMATCH ANALYSIS

For the position of: Data Processor and Programmer
From the writing of: Female–age 42–left handed

TRAIT Requirement	Handwriting Factor	Degree of Use Strong	Medium	Weak/none
Organization	Consistent margins	x		
	Balanced f		x	
	Even baseline	x		
Creativity	Picture value		x	
Initiative	No beginning strokes	x		
	Long t crosses	x		
Independence	Left slant	x		
	"Stick" capital I	x		
Objectivity	Simple letter form	x		
Judgment	Margins defined	x		
	Left slant	x		
	Straight baseline	x		
Self Confidence	Consistent MZH	x		
	Long capital I	x		
	Underlined signature	Not available		
Determination	Heavy, straight downstrokes	x		
Physical Stamina	Pressure		x	
	Fullness			x
	LZ length	x		
Logic	Connected letters		x	x
Analysis	Organization	x		
	Simple letters	x		
Versatile	Both printed and cursive letters	x		
Mechanical	Printed caps	x		
	Figures well formed		x	
Common Sense	Straight baseline	x		
	Consistency	x		
	Original forms	x		
Loyalty	Precise i dots	x		
	High t cross	x		
Eye oriented	Details	x		
	Picture value		x	
	MZH		x	
	TOTALS	24	6	3

Evaluation:

Positive 24 out of 33 factors equals 72.7%
Medium 6 out of 33 factors equals 18.2%
Weak/None 3 out of 33 factors equals 9.1%

HONESTY EVALUATION
From the writing of: Female–age 42–left handed

Note: At least five dishonest factors must be consistently repeated to judge a writing dishonest.

Honest	Strong	Medium	Medium	Strong	Dishonest
Even baseline	x				Uneven baseline
Firm pressure				x	Light/varied pressure
Right tendencies				x	Left tendencies
Legibility		x			Illegibility
Free movement			x		Cramped, retraced
Short initials	x				Initial hooks
Even MZ height	x				Uneven MZ "Jump-up" letters
Conservative Capital I			x		Extreme Capital I
Consistency	x				Inconsistency
Ovals clear	x				Ovals
					Embellished
					Looped—left
					Looped—right
					Doubled looped
					Open at bottom
TOTALS	5	1	2	2	

Degree of Honesty (column group header spanning Strong/Medium/Medium/Strong)

Evaluation: Strong sense of honesty and loyalty
Good risk

Follow-up Report on Ms. C.

Hired on our recommendation, Ms. C. worked for four months
to the end of the project. She often worked ten or more hours to
meet deadlines. She declined to sign up for a subsequent project, on advice of her physician, but after a three-months rest
she did sign for a similar but less demanding project. Her superiors plan to employ her as often as her health allows.

SUMMARY OF THE OCCUPATIONAL PERSONALITY

From the writing of: female, age 42, left handed

Company: Government Contract Company

Recommendation: Hire

Basic Personality: This writer's script shows she is a very reserved personality, above average intellect, capable and consisent in all she does. Not especially warm or outgoing where personal affairs are concerned, in a business world, she has the cultural training to present herself in a poised and efficient manner. She sets her goals and pursues them with determination and without waste of time or energy. She is more of a mental person than a woman of physical pursuits.

Honesty and Loyalty on the Job: This writer is quite capable of the necessary loyalty required for this top secret clearance job. She has a deep sense of personal pride which would not allow her to betray a confidence.

She is one who wastes neither time nor materials. In her personal affairs she is relatively thrifty and probably has developed some kind of long-range security program.

Work Habits: The peculiar requirement for a programmer who can work alone and especially one who can accept being locked into a security base during working hours seems to hold little problem for this writer. She can think independently, therefore needs little supervision. She is capable of solving the normal problems that occur in a job of this kind with ingenuity, versatility and common sense.

Her physical stamina is limited which may make it necessary for her to take regular breaks. She tends to push herself on nervous energy when stressed. However, her ability to work alone relieves her of the need to relate to others so she can pace herself according to the workload.

She is well organized, and if kept apprised of what is required she will be able to fulfill whatever is asked of her. She is generally cheerful and willing to cooperate, even to be imposed upon at times. However, she will state her needs if she feels abused.

Recommendation: This woman is well qualified emotionally and intellectually to fill the job requirements as outlined. It is assumed her computer skills have already been evaluated and meet the needs of the company. The weak spot is her physical stamina, but with common sense she should be able to arrange her work to complete what is asked of her in an adequate time frame.

Travel Agent and Office Manager

Handwriting Analysis requirements from: International Travel

From the writing of: Gayle–Female–Age 44–Right Handed

Description of Company:

An international travel company that franchises small offices throughout many cities. Each office has from three to twenty employees including Office Manager, Customer Services, Bookkeeper, and as many clerk-agents as needed.

All employees are geared toward serving the public, at the same time they must deal with computerized information used by many different airlines. Certain individuals may also be required to act as tour guide on bus, train or plane trips.

Description of position to be filled: Travel agent and office manager

Requirements of position	Personality traits
1. Must be able to handle the public as well as airline needs.	a. cheerful b. patient c. friendly
2. Needs computer skills.	a. manual dexterity b. logical c. organized
3. Will have independent working conditions without supervision.	a. confident b. organized c. initiative
4. Must work with machines telex, ticket machine etc.	a. mechanical b. patience
5. Must solve complex problems in logistics.	a. flexible b. versatile c. resourceful
6. Must work with data details and timing.	a. good memory b. precise
7. Must provide specific services for sometimes difficult clients.	a. listening skills b. persuasive c. ability to compromise
8. Must show business profit.	a. practical b. precision with numbers.
9. Must supervise several employees, both men and women.	a. decisive b. firm ego c. fair

BASIC FACTORS ANALYSIS

For the position of: Travel agent and officer manager
From the writing of: Gayle–Female–Age 44–Right Handed

Basics of handwriting **Comments**

- PICTURE VALUE — Clear, pleasant to look at, conventional
- SLANT
  - Firm — Friendly
  - Rightward — Compliant
- BASELINE
  - Even, slight upslant — Dependable, Optimistic
- MARGINS
  - Consistently even — Fits into her environment well
  - Left narrow, — Slightly shy
    - slight right drift — —Capable of overcoming shyness
  - Right — Cautious
    - wide, even — —Consistent
- SIZE
  - Medium — Conventional, normal self esteem
  - MZ
    - even — Consistent, goal directed
    - medium — Good general worker
  - UZ-LZ
    - good proportion — Practical, well organized
    - balanced *fs* — Can plan as well as executive plans
  - Loops
    - narrow — Works on nervous energy
    - long, open — Good for office work routine
- SPACE
  - Expansion
    - normal — Can take—and give—directions
  - Between lines
    - wide, no overlaps — Clear thinking, organized
  - Between words
    - wide — Needs time and privacy to organize complex problems
- PRESSURE
  - Light to normal — Easy to get along with
  - — Needs periods of privacy
- SPEED
  - Normal — Takes her time with details
  - — Handles time by good planning and efficient methods
- CLARITY (legibility)
  - Excellent — Communicates with others well
  - — Listens to others

April 23, 1987

Dear Eldine & Bob,

Here is your package for your England vacation. How wonderful it all sounds. I know you'll have a great time. Just being with Dee & Kent will make it an entirely different trip for you. Included in your package are your airline tickets, your vouchers for the London Explorer pass and your confirmation and contract for the car rental. Your hotel documents should be in any day now. I'll call you as soon as they arrive.

Have a wonderful time.

Love,
Gayle

Female–Age 44–Right Handed

TRAITMATCH ANALYSIS

For the position of: Travel Agent and Officer Manager
From the writing of: Gayle–female–age 44–right handed

Trait Requirement	Handwriting Factor	Strong	Medium	Weak/none
Cheerful	Upslant baseline		x	
	Round letter form	x		
Patient	Precise letter form	x		
	Curved endings		x	
Friendly	Left margin drifts		x	
	Right slant	x		
	Round form	x		
Manual dexterity	Squared r	x		
Logic	Connected letters	x		
	Consistent pressure		x	
Organization	Balanced f loops		x	
	Even baselines	x		
	Consistent margins	x		
Confidence	Large capitals		x	
	Consistent MZH	x		
	Underlined signature			x
Initiative	Long t bars	x		
	No beginning strokes		x	
Mechanical	Printed capitals			x
	Clear numbers	x		
Flexible	Speed		x	
	Right slant	x		
	Round writing	x		
Versatile	Printing + Cursive			x
	Original form		x	
Resourceful	Original form		x	
	High t bars, i dots		x	
	Open LZ loops		x	
Memory	Precise t bars, i dots	x		
	Legible script	x		
	Small MZ		x	
Precise	Careful t bars i dots	x		
	Clear, neat script	x		
Listening skills	Neat, careful script	x		
	Round form	x		
	Complete endings		x	
Persuasive	Original script		x	
	Strong t bars	x		
	MZH diminishes			x

		Strong	Medium	Weak
Ability to compromise	Round script	x		
	Varied pressure		x	
Practical	Short UZH	x		
	Printing			x
	Round MZ ovals		x	
Money skills	Clear numbers	x		
	Low *t* bars		x	
Decisive	Firm *t* bars	x		
	Large capitals	x		
	Firm finals		x	
Ego	Large capitals	x		
	Firm pressure		x	
	Long LZ loops	x		
Fair	Round MZ ovals	x		
	Firm *t* bars	x		
	Large capitals	x		
TOTALS		29	20	5

Positive 29 out of 54 factors equals 55%
Medium 20 out of 54 factors equals 36%
Weak/none 5 out of 54 factors equals 9%

HONESTY EVALUATION

From the writing of: Gayle–female–age 44–right handed

Note: At least five dishonest factors must be consistently repeated to judge a writing dishonest.

Honest	Strong	Medium	Medium	Strong	Dishonest
		Degree of Honesty			
Even baseline	x				Uneven baseline
Firm pressure		x			Light, varied pressure
Right tendency	x				Left tendency
Legibility	x				Illegibility
Free movement		x			Cramped, retraced, slow
Short initials		x		x	Initial hooks, claw
Even MZ height	x				Uneven MZ "Jump-up" letters
Copybook Cap I	x				Extremes in Cap I
Consistency	x				Inconsistency
Ovals clear	x				Ovals
					Embellished
					Looped–left
					Looped–right
					Doubled looped
					Open at bottom
TOTALS	7	3		1	

EVALUATION: Excellent honesty

SUMMARY OF OCCUPATIONAL PERSONALITY
From the writing of: Gayle–female–age 44–right handed
Recommendation: Promote to office manager

Basic Personality: This woman is a conventional and conservative personality who makes every effort to be friendly and pleasant. Reserved and shy on first contact, she gives a good impression of knowing what she is doing. She has a good sense of humor and a willingness to go out of her way to accommodate others.

Work Habits: She is very well organized and can handle routine work with cheerful dispatch. Not always original or innovative she uses practical and previously tried solutions to everyday problems. At times her good humor may be taken advantage of, but once she feels she is being imposed on she will balk, extricating herself with tact and firmness. Confrontations upset her, so she is tolerant and polite in an effort to avoid them. At the same time she will set out the desired conduct for those she supervises to satisfy the needs of the office. She is not aggressive, but she is assertive.

Her attention to detail is an asset to an office that demands many details to run smoothly. She can quickly spot a problem with an employee, a bookkeeping error or an error with computer data. What cannot be solved immediately, she will work on mentally until she finds an answer. She has been disappointed in the past by actions of others, so she is suspicious of a snag until she finds the cause.

Physical Attributes: Gayle is neat in her work and probably very careful in her dress. She makes a good appearance for making presentations. Stamina is not very strong, but her sense of organization and priority provides a good substitute.

She is capable of doing all the types of work in a travel office including operating the typewriter, computer and photography equipment. She understands what happens when things go wrong and can offer practical suggestions for alternate action.

Honesty: Her honesty is absolute. With only one factor in the negative column, she has very strong values and will insist on integrity from those under her. Her ethics are firm, conservative and conventional.

Practical requirements: Because she is both practical and pragmatic, Gayle can handle most of the clients who come to her office. She has past experience as both bookkeeper and clerk, and her six years experience with all phases of travel agent work gives her the practical knowledge to help her office employees in peak periods. She doesn't mind hard work, and has no illusions about being "better than anyone else."

Recommendation: Gayle has an excellent personality for the type of work demand of both a travel agent and an office manager. She is conservative enough to follow orders from the home office, yet firm enough in her own ego to guide office personnel. At times it may be easier for her to do the job than to explain it to another, but she also has the objectivity to delegate work when necessary.

Her warm personality will create an atmosphere that will encourage clients to return to her office because they like her and know she has their interests at heart. For this same reason her employees will like her as a person and know she will stand by their judgments.

We recommend that Gayle be promoted to office manager.

Follow-up Report on Gayle.

Gayle was promoted on our recommendation. Her previous six years' experience as a travel agent was extremely valuable in maintaining a strong net profit for the company. After one year we checked her progress and learned that she had improved the office gross by 30 per cent through practical advertising and careful follow up.

Her superiors are encouraging her now to open a new office in another part of the city as a franchise. She recognizes the risk of buying into the venture, but expects to apply the same practical and ethical methods to insure success in her own business.

Administrative Assistant

Handwriting Analysis requirements from: ABC School District

From the writing of: Robert L.G.–Male–age 45–Right Handed

Description of Company:

At the request of the writer, Robert L. G., the ABC School District asked for an analysis of his handwriting to help establish his potential as an administrative assistant within the district. He has been a first grade teacher for fourteen years and wants a change.

The school district is a large one in a mid-west state. There are many administrative assistants within the district who receive information from state offices to be disseminated and administered in each district. The job also calls for working out new and often unpopular programs with principals at individual schools. This particular district also sends administrative assistants to referee complaints of parents with teachers and principals.

Description of position to be filled: Administrative Assistant

Requirements of position	Personality traits
1. Must act as liaison between disagree- parties.	a. diplomacy b. patience c. listening skills
2. Must understand practical business procedures.	a. organization b. logic c. analysis
3. Must adapt to new concepts and explain them to others.	a. flexible b. open minded c. compliance
4. Must solve problems within the district structure.	a. versatile b. initiative c. firm ego
5. May be required to make speeches and present new ideas.	a. persuasive b. verbal facility c. confidence
6. Must be willing to work unusual hours.	a. physical stamina b. health c. compliance

BASIC FACTORS ANALYSIS

For the position of: Administrative Assistant
From the writing of: Robert L.G.–Male–Age 44–Right Handed

Basics of handwriting   Comments

- PICTURE VALUE
  Clear, legible   Willing to communicate, organized
- SLANT
  Medium right slant   Compliant, outgoing, capable of meeting people
- BASELINE
  Even, slight upslant   Dependable, optimistic, usually cheerful
- MARGINS
  Medium, slight right drift   Conservative, interested in others
- SIZE
  MZ
    Medium size, even   Conventional
    Consistent MZH   Firm ego
  UZ versus LZ
    Normal proportions   Conforms to norm
    Good balance in f's   Organized, practical
  Medium UZ   Practical ideas
  Medium LZ   Physical stability
  Loops
    Medium to full UZ and   Fair imagination
    LZ   Conventional ideas
- SPACE
  Expansion   Needs space to work in
    Wide MZ letters   Doesn't like close supervision
  Between lines
    Lines separated, no   Clear thinking, but reserved
    touching
  Word space is open,   Good social instincts
  even
- PRESSURE
  Mixed light and heavy   Inconsistent energy level
  downstrokes   Determined, decisive
- SPEED (legibility)
  Medium to slow   Needs time to organize
- CLARITY (legibility)   Deliberates over decisions
  Excellent   Good communicator
                                Uncomplicated thinker

TRAITMATCH ANALYSIS
For the position of: Administrative Assistant
From the writing of: Robert L G.–Male–Age 44–Right Handed

Trait Requirement	Handwriting Factor	Degree of use		
		Strong	Medium	Weak/none
Diplomacy	Decreasing letter size			x
	Pressure		x	
Patience	Round letters		x	
	Neat, clear	x		
	Careful *i* dots	x		
Listening skills	Neat Script	x		
	Round form		x	
	Complete endings	x		
Organization	Margin spacing		x	
	Balanced *f* loops	x		
	Consistent slant	x		
	Consistent pressure		x	
Logic	Connected letters	x		
	Consistent pressure		x	
Analysis	Printing			x
	Angles		x	
Flexible	Round, clear	x		
	Right slant	x		
	Even baseline	x		
Open minded	Round ovals		x	
	Clear ovals	x		
Compliant	Garlands	x		
	Right slant	x		
Versatile	Varied forms			x
	Printed and cursive	x		
Firm ego	Large caps	x		
	Pressure		x	
	Long LZ loops		x	
Persuasive	Original script			x
	Strong *t* bars		x	
	Diminished MZH			x
Verbal facility	Ovals, some open	x		
	Some closed			
	Right slant	x		
Confidence	Consistent MZH	x		
	Capital *I*		x	
	Underlined signature			x
Physical stamina	Pressure		x	
	Fullness		x	
	LZ length		x	
TOTALS		18	15	6

163

EVALUATION:
Positive 18 out of 39 factors equals 46%
Medium 15 out of 39 factors equals 39%
Weak/none 6 out of 39 factors equals 16%

SUMMARY OF OCCUPATIONAL PERSONALITY
From the writing of: Robert L.G.–Male–Age 44–Right Handed
Recommendation: Adequate qualifications for administrative assistant, but better as a teacher of elementary grades

Basic Personality: Robert L.G's writing shows an excellent personality for teaching young children, and less ability for the demanding needs of adult administration. He is friendly and outgoing. As a caring individual he answers the needs of youngsters. He is cheerful and caring but he can be firm, applying his personal consistency and conservative approach to daily tasks. His optimism and dependability are great assets in the world of elementary school traditions.

Honesty: Honesty was not a question in this analysis.

Work Habits: While this man's writing shows diplomacy, patience, organization and flexibility, his emotional approach to the problems of the complex needs within a school district would make it difficult for him to implement new and innovative laws and to translate them into practical use.

His compliance and flexibility as well as his desire to be liked tend to cause him to solve problems with his feelings rather than cold facts. Confronted by a strong willed arguer, he could be persuaded to change his decisions. This same adaptability is a strong asset in carrying out the requests of both principals and administrators, but his ego is not strong enough to withstand sustained criticism, rough arguments or personal accusations. He likes to get along with everyone.

Social Skills: Mr. L.G. has the normal social skills required of a school executive, and his general likeability would help him a great deal in the social functions required of an administrative assistant. But he is not a highly cultured, academic or innovative person, preferring the conventional scene.

Recommendation: While Mr. L.G. has many of the necessary requirements for an administrative assistant, we recommend that he stay in his present job as elementary school teacher. His personality is very well suited for dealing with children, a rather rare quality in our present day schools. These talents would be lost in a job that could prove to be both frustrating and stressful for the client.

Follow-up Report:
   Despite our report Mr. L.G. decided to apply for the job of administrative assistant and he was hired on a probationary contract of one year. Before the year was up, however, he recognized the wisdom of our analysis. During a routine health appraisal he learned that his blood pressure increased. He did not enjoy the personal contacts he made during the year. Although his superiors were satisfied with his work, he realized he would not be happy in this work as a long term career, and did not renew his contract. Fortunately, there was still a place for him in his old school which he accepted.

10 July 1987

Greetings Eldene,

Will you please do a complete analysis of my handwriting? I would like to gain insight into the direction I should take with my career. I would like you to offer me as many suggestions as possible in this area. Futher-more would you please point out any of my naturally strong areas?

Would you please let me know what your fees for this will be and I will send you a check at once.

My best wishes for a wonderful summer!

Sincerely,
Robert L. G

Male–Age 44–Right Handed

APPENDIX II

HISTORY OF GRAPHOLOGY

A chronological development of graphology through the people who have contributed to its progress.

OBSERVERS OF HANDWRITING
1000 B.C.
Japanese scholars judged that character conformed to the way a man traces his bars according to the thickness, length, ridigity or suppleness.

300 B.C.
ARISTOTLE: Philosopher (Greece)
"Spoken words are the symbols of mental experience and written words are the symbols of spoken words. Just as all men have not the same speech sounds, so all men have not the same writing."

120 A.D.
SUETONIUS TRANQUILLUS: Historian (Roman Empire)
Describing the writing of Emperor Augustus said: "I have above all remarked the following in his writing. He does not separate his words, nor does he carry over to the next line any excess letters; instead he places them under the final word and ties them to it with a stroke."

400 A.D.
JUSTINIAN: Emperor (Roman Empire)
Impressed by the change in a handwriting with the changes in health and the advancement of old age.

1060-1110 A.D.
KUO JO HSU: Philosopher, painter of Sung period (China)
"Handwriting infallibly shows us whether it comes from a vulgar or a noble minded person."

ADVANCERS OF GRAPHOLOGY
1600s
ALDERISUIS PROSPER: Physician (Italy)
Published a study called "Ideographia" showing a systematic relationship between handwriting and personality traits.

1662
CAMILLO BALDI: Professor, philosophy, medicine (Italy)
Published a study presenting a first method for judging a writer's nature from his letter formations.

1700s
SHELLY AYERS and other English writing masters developed the Round Hand technique of writing which included flourishs, curved loops and ligatures. This style encouraged speed and fluency in writing.

1792
J. CHARLES GROHMANN: Professor, theology, philosophy (Germany)
Published treatise: "Examination of the possibility of Inferring Character from Handwriting."

1830
ABBE FLANDRIN: Priest, teacher (France)
Collected for thirty years thousands of writings and classified them by "elements of design in handwriting." Interpretation was a trait-for-a-stroke method.

1860
HAVELOCK ELLIS: Psychologist (England)
Used graphology to study the criminal mind. Worked with Alphonse Bertillon who developed identification through finger-prints and Sir William Herschel who stressed the importance of character deduction through criminology.

1872
ABBE JEAN HIPPOLYTE MICHON: Priest, teacher (France)
Coined the word "graphology". Published two very popular books. "Les Mysteres de l'ecriture" 1872 and "La Methode practique de graphologie" in 1878. In these the law of balance was formulated stressing a blending of interpretations.

1888-1924
JEAN CREPIEUX-JAMIN: Psychologist (France)
The first "scientific graphologist". Developed the theory of resultants which stressed that the whole writing must be considered. Still used in French graphology.

1890
ROSA BAUGHN: Author (England)
Wrote the first graphology book in English, "Character Indicated by Handwriting."

1895
WILHELM PREYER: Professor, physiology (Germany)
Discovered the similarity of writing done with the left hand, right hand, toes or teeth. Called all writing 'brain writing' to demonstrate the central origination of all writing.

1896
GEORGE MEYER: Psychiatrist (Germany)
Developed a much needed characterology and a common vocabulary. Relationship between movement of writing and emotion as psychomotor energy.

1898
ALFRED BINET: Psychologist (France)
Did the first research on age and sex of writers. Results class these as physical factors not revealed by handwriting alone.

1905
LUDWIG KLAGES: Ph.D Philosopher (Germany)
Considered to be the founder of modern graphology. Combined all previous methods into a "Science of Expression." Developed the principals of "Formnivea" (Form level) and rhythm.

1908
LOUISE RICE: Newswoman (New York City)
Caused a postal law to be written that no mail of a graphologist could be stopped on grounds of 'fortune telling.'

1910
EMIL KRAEPELIN: Psychiatrist (Germany)
Experimented in measurement of pressure and speed in the writing of normal and disturbed persons using his Kraepelin scale.

1912
LOUISE RICE: Newswoman (New York City)
Wrote the first newspaper column on graphology.

1919
JUNE DOWNEY: Psychologist, teacher (University of Iowa)
Published "Graphology and the Psychology of Handwriting." Taught the first graphology course in an American college.

1920
KLARA ROMAN: Ph.D Psychologist (Hungary)
Developed the psychogram as a method for measuring graphology factors. Invented the graphodyne to measure speed and pressure. Wrote "Handwriting, a Key to Personality," considered a leading textbook for modern American graphologists.

1920's
BERNARD WITTLICH: Psychologist (Germany)
Developed a measuring scale and published manuals for students of medical, criminology and psychology classes.

1920's
MAX PULVER: Philosopher (Switzerland)
Developed the use of three zones in writing. Upper zone—abstract thinking; middle zone—emotion; lower zone—biological factors.

1930's
GORDON ALLPORT, PHILIP VERNON: Psychologists (Harvard Psychological Clinic)
Investigated expressive movement and added validity to graphology by including it in their tests.

1930's
ROBERT SAUDEK: Graphologist (England)
Contributed a thorough research and analysis of the different types of penmanship. Developed a criteria for discovering dishonesty in writing. Founded the first journal of graphology "Character and Personality".

1939
HANS J. JACOBY wrote a textbook, "Analysis of Handwriting" bringing the European method of analysis to England and America.

1940
LUDWIG KLAGES: Ph.D Philosopher (Germany)
Wrote "Handshrift and Charakter," used as classic text in European universities.

1942
THEA STEIN LEWINSON, JOSEPH ZUBIN: Psychologists (Ann Arbor, Michigan
Developed a seven point system of scales to measure the balance of contraction and release in handwriting.

1942
WERNER WOLFF: Graphologist (America)
Published "Diagrams of the Unconscious" to prove the consistency of personality as shown in the signature throughout one's life.

1945
MAX PULVER: Professor of Psychology (Switzerland)
Wrote "Symbolik der Handschrift" which broadened graphic interpretations by applying psychoanalytical methods of Freud, Adler, Jung and Steckel.

1949
ULRICH SONNEMAN: Ph.D (New York)
Conducted research projects using handwriting analysis in the New School for Social Research, New York City. His findings contributed to the use of graphology in clinical psychology.

1949
ROSE WOLFSON: Psychologist (Ann Arbor, Michigan)
Found significant differences between writings of delinquent and non-delinquent persons.

1954

RUDOLPH POPHAL: Neurologist and Ph.D (Germany)
Founded a Graphological Research Institute in Hamburg, Germany with Wilhelm Preyer, Professor of Physiology. Studied handwriting as "brain writing" as reflected in physiological movements of tension and release.

1954

THEWLIS, Dr. M.W. and Swezy, Isabelle C. (Wakefield, R.I.)
Wrote "Handwriting and the Emotions," an in-depth study of nervous diseases and the effects of the emotions on handwriting.

1960s

CHARLIE COLE: Analyst and teacher (San Jose, California)
Organized and promoted graphology by holding seminars with the "names" prominent in graphology. Later founded the American Handwriting Analysis Foundation, and directed the Handwriting Analysis Workshops Unlimited, a professional school for in-house and correspondence students.

1961

AXEL SJOBERG, Graphologist (Saskatchewan, Canada)
Began publication of The Canadian Analyst, which has served a widely scattered group of graphologists in the U.S. and Canada from all schools of analytical teachings. Still in circulation as of 1987.

1965

ALFRED KANFER, Graphologist
Developed a magnification system (enlarged 500 to 1000 times) for discovering the early signs of cancer in the writing stroke. Worked for 30 years with the Hospital for Joint Diseases and for Strang Clinic in New York. Was 85 per cent accurate.

1966

PAUL de STE. COLOME: Philosopher (France)
Introduced into the United States a method of changing the handwriting to change the personality called "Grapho-Therapeutics."

1966
ROBERT HEISS, Ph.D. (Germany)
Director of the Institute for Psychology and Characterology at the University of Freiburg, Germany. Handwriting Analysis used in the cirriculum. Heiss organized handwriting into "Space, Form and Movement" and stated that all writing factors can be arranged under these headings. He wrote "Die Deutung der Handschrift."

1969
ROBERT BACKMAN: Curator of Handwriting Analysis Research Library (Massachusetts)
Founded the library in 1949; incorporated in 1969. Has collected more than 70,000 graphological items, catalogued and made them available to students and researchers.

1969
RHODA KELLOG: Educator (California)
Developed an analysis of children's art that added to graphological information on the symbolism found in writing. Wrote "Analyzing Children's Art."

1971
BETTY LINK, DR. WILLIAM HALLOW
First Accreditation for certifying qualified graphologists developed through American Association of Handwriting Analysts. On the West Coast the American Handwriting Analysis Foundation followed suit.

1972
BETTY LINK C.G.
Published "Graphology, a Tool for Personnel Selection," the first time handwriting analysis for business was put into one volume.

1975
SHAFIR, A. HIRSCH, M. & SHEPPS S.: Psychologists (Israel)
First used graphology in conjunction with Bender, Gestalt, Draw-a-Person and Rorschach testing methods in a research project using Jewish victims of the Holocaust, 1940-1945.

1978
HELEN DINKLAGE C.G.: Therapist, Counselor (California)
A registed Music Therapist and Psychodramatist, she was Director of Creative Art Therapies for nearly 20 years in U.S. mental hospitals. Wrote "Therapy Through Handwriting."

1979
JACQUELINE PEGEOT: Educator (France)
Write "La Conn de l'enfant par 'ecriture" (Knowledge of the child through Handwriting).

1980
DR. ERIKA M. KAROHS
Translated European graphology works of Max Pulver, Rhoda Weiser, Rudolf Pophal, Pokorny and Wittlich among others. Her Encyclopedia for Handwriting Analysts is an extensive work.

1980
PAULA SASSI C.G., ELDENE WHITING C.G. (San Diego, Calif.) As Handwriting Consultants International wrote four courses using an eclectic approach to handwriting analysis and incorporating general psychology with emphasis on Jung. Courses offered world wide on a commercial basis.

1982
ROSE MATOUSEK: Graphologist (Illinois)
Instrumental in convincing the Library of Congress to take Graphology from the occult designation and put it into its rightful place under psychology.

1982
BARBERA MC MENAMIN C.G., GLORIA VADUS C.G., ELDENE WHITING C.G.
Research project on printing. Wrote "An Investigation of Cursive Versus Printing Characteristics in Handwriting."

1983
FELIX KLEIN (New York City)
Translated some of the works of both Ludwig Klages and Max Pulver into English for American use.

1986
BETTY LINK C.G.
Published "Advanced Graphology," a text book on practical methods for handwriting analysis.

1986
BETTY SEMLER-DELMAR
Published "Schematic Graphology," a textbook on the Wittlich method of handwriting analysis measurements.

Appendix III

GRAPHOLOGICAL SOCIETIES

American Graphological Society
1913-1967
Founder, Louise Rice, newspaperwoman, New York City

American Association of Handwriting Analysts
1963 to present. Founding member of Council of Graphological Societies
Founder, Carroll Chouinard, graphologist, Chicago, Illinois

American Association of Professional Graphologists
1986 to present
Founder, Thea Stein Lewinson, New York City

American Handwriting Analysis Foundation
1967 to present. Founding member of Council of Graphological Societies.
Founder, Charlie Cole, graphologist. Director of Handwriting Analysis Workshop Unlimited, a correspondence and residence school based on the Klara Roman psychogram. San Jose, Calif.

Calumet Association of Handwriting Analysts
1973 to present. Charter member-group of Council of Graphological Societies.
Founder, Martha Brown C.G. (Hammond, Indiana)

Council of Graphological Societies
1972 to present
Founded by the combined efforts of the boards of the American Association of Handwriting Analysts and the American Handwriting Analysis Foundation. Open to all organized groups of handwriting analysts.
Charter President, Elva Babcock

Eastern Graphological Organization
Founder, Stan Vidinghoff, Rochester, New York

Great Lakes Association of Handwriting Examiners
1986 to present
Charter President, Ruth Holmes, Bloomfield Hills, Michigan

Handwriting Analysts International
President, Jean Peterson, Euclid, Ohio

International Graphoanalysis Society
1929 to present
A correspondence school of GraphoAnalysis (trademark) based on the gestalt school of handwriting analysis.
Founder, M.N. Bunker, Shorthand Teacher Springfield, Missouri
V. Peter Ferrara M.A. continued the commercial venture at the death of Bunker. (Chicago, Illinois)

The Institute of Graphological Sciences
Founded 1983
Founder, Mary Lynn Bryden Ph.D. (Dallas, Texas)
First school to be licensed by a state.

National Association of Document Examiners
1980 to present
Founder, Phyllis Cook MGA
Charter President, Renee C. Martin, Glenside, Pennsylvania

National Society of Graphologists
1972 to present. Member of Council of Graphological Soc.
Founder, Felix Klein, Graphologist, New York City

New England Institute for the Study of Handwriting Analysis
1986 to present
Founder, Jean Caya Bancroft, Wellesley Hills, Massachusetts

Rocky Mountain Graphology Association
1975 to present
Founder, Gwen Sampson, Denver, Colorado

Society of Handwriting Analysts
1970 to present
Founder, Dr. David Mayer, Washington, D.C.

Western Society of Graphology and Graphotherapeutics
1985 to present
Founder, Freda Miller, Fort Dick, California

World Association of Document Examiners
Associated with IGAS, Chicago, Illinois

FOREIGN COUNTRY ORGANIZATIONS

Asociacion Grafopsicologia
Pez 27–1 dcha 28004 Madrid, Spain

Association des Graphologues
13400 Est Sainte Catherine
C.P. 215 Succ.C, Montreal, Quebec H2L 4K1, Canada

Associazione Grafologica Italiana
Via Oberdan 3; 60122 Ancona C.P. 178, Italia

Berufsverband Geprufter Graphologen/Psychologen e.V
Sitz Muchen, Cimbernstrasse 70 C
8000 Munchen 70, West Germany

British Institute of Graphologists
119 b Priory Rd. West Hampstead, London NW6 3NN, England

Canadian Graphology Consultants Association
908-1729 Barclay Street, Vancouver, B.C. V6G 1K4, Canada

Federation Nationale des Graphologues Professionnels
2 bis rue Roger Simon Barboux, 94110 Arcueil, France

Internationale Gesellschaft fur Dynamische und Klinische Schriftpsychologie-DKS
Erlenweg 14; D7000 Stuttgart 70, West Germany

Instituto Grafologico "Girolamo Moretti"
Piazza San Francesco 7
61029 Urbino, Italy

Saskatchewan Handwriting Analysis Club
4910 Avenue W North; Saskatoon, Saskatchewan, Canada

Syndicat des Graphologues Professionels
5 bis Boulevard des Italiens
75005 Oaris, France

SCHOOLS OF GRAPHOLOGY

The Academy of Graphology
Renna Nezos, Principal
1 Queens Elm Square, London SW3 6ED, England

Association for Graphological Studies
Rose Toomey, Director
13092 Caminito Del Rocio, Del Mar, CA 92014

The Graphology Center
Sheila Lowe, Director
11740 Courtleigh Dr., Los Angeles, CA 90066

Handwriting Analysis Workshop Unlimited
Dr. Ellen Bowers, Director
5564 Millington Rd., Columbus, OH 43220

Handwriting Consultants International
Paula Sassi, Director
11481 Caminito Garcia, San Diego, CA 92131

Humananalysis Institute
A.D. Hartmark, Director
1280 West Highway 96, St. Paul, MN 55112

Institut Canadien de Caracterologie
D.A. Gauthier, Director
1340 Est Ste Catherine, C.P. 214 Succ C
Montreal, Quebec, Canada H2L 4K1

Institut International de Recherches Graphologigues
Le Pave du Roy, 77780 Bourron Marlotte, France

Institute of Graphological Research
Diane Seaman, Director
610 Lochmoor Court, Danville, CA 94526

Institute of Graphological Science
Mary Lynn, Bryden, Founder and Director
3685 Ingleside, Dallas, TX 75229

New School for Social Research
1948 to present
Founders, Ulrich Sonneman and Klara Roman
Teachers, 1968–1980: Daniel and Florence Anthony
           1980 to present: Pat Seigal and Lois Vaisman
The first to develop a fully accredited college curriculum of eight
semesters of handwriting analysis.

SELECTED REFERENCES

ADLER, A., *Understanding Human Nature*, New York: Greenberg, 1946

ALLPORT, G.; VERNON, P., *Studies in Expressive Movement*, New York: Macmillan, 1933

BATTAN, DAVID, *Handwriting Analysis: A Guide to Personality*, Pismo Beach, CA: International Resources, 1984.

BROWNE, H., *How I Found Freedom in an Unfree World*, New York: Macmillan, 1973

CARNEGIE, D. & Assoc., *Managing Through People*, New York: Simon and Schuster, 1975

CECIL, E.A.; PAUL, R.J.; OLINS, R.A., Perceived Importance of Selected Variables used to Evaluate Male and Female Job Applicants. *Personnel Psychology*, Vol. 26, 1976

COLE, C.; HARTMAN, J., *Criteria*, San Jose, CA: Handwriting Analysis Workshop Unlimited, 1975

CURRIER-BRIGGS, N.; KENNETT, B.; PATTERSON, J., *Handwriting Analysis in Business*, Bath, England: Pitman Press, 1971

ELSNER, D., Job Applications are Trickier Than Ever: Mind Your P'S and Q'S. *Wall Street Journal*, June 20, 1974

FAST, J., *Body Language*, New York: M. Evans and Company, 1970

FULLMER, T., The Use of Graphoanalysis in Personnel Selection. *Best's Review* (Life Edition), June 1971

GARDNER, J., Handwriting Analysis Finds Growing Favor in Personnel Offices. *Wall Street Journal*, Sept. 11, 1967

GULLEN-WHUR, MARGARET, *What Your Handwriting Reveals*, Northamptonshire, England: Aquarian press, 1984.

HARTFORD, H., *You Are What You Write*, New York: Macmillan, 1973

HEARNS, R., *Handwriting and Analysis Through its Symbolism*, New York: Vantage Press, 1966

HERMAN, S., *The People Specialists*, New York: Alfred Knopf, 1968

HOLDER, R., *Handwriting Talks*, New York: Farnsworth, 1974

———*Sex, Health and Your Handwriting*, New York: Award, 1971

HUNT, P.; HORTON, C., *Sociology,* New York: McGraw-Hill, 1972

IRISH, R., *If Things Don't Improve Soon, I May Ask You to Fire Me.,* Garden City, N.Y.: Anchor Press, 1975

JACOBY, H., *Analysis of Handwriting,* London, England: George Allen & Unwin, Ltd., 1968

JANSEN, A., *Validation of Graphological Judgements: An Experimental Study,* The Hague, Netherlands: Mouton, 1973

JOURNAL, International Grapho-Analysis Society, Chicago, III: November 1975

JUNG, C., *Man and His Symbols,* New York: Doubleday, 1964

KAROHS, ERIKA C.G., *Handwriting Analysis—Step by Step Profit Guide,* Pebble Beach, CA, 1979.

———*Occupational Trait Inventory,* Pebble Beach, CA 1976.

KATZ, R., Skills of an Effective Administrator. *Harvard Business Review,* Sept. 1974

KURDSEN, S., *Graphology, The New Science,* New York: Galahad, 1971

LINDBERG, ELAYNE, *The Power of Positive Handwriting,* Staples, MN: Adventure Publications, 1987.

LINK, B., *Graphology, A Tool for Personnel Selection,* Minneapolis, Minn.: Paul S. Amidone & Assoc., 1972

LINK, BETTY C.G., *Advanced Graphology,* Chicago: Personsel Consultants & Publishers Inc., 1987.

LOENGARD, M., *How to Analyze Your Handwriting,* London, England: Marshall Cavendish, 1975

MAIER, N., *Psychology in Industrial Organizations,* Boston, Mass: Houghton Mifflin, 1973

MARCUSE, I., *Guide to Personality Through Your Handwriting,* New York: Arco, 1971

McNEAL, J. Graphology: A New Marketing Research Technique, *Journal of Marketing Research,* Vol. IV, November 1967

MENDEL, A., *Personality in Handwriting,* New York: Stephen Daye Press, 1971

MEYERS, J., More on Graphology and Marketing: An Empirical Validation of Marketing Graphology, *Journal of American Research,* Vol. VI, February 1969

MEYER, J., *Mind Your P'S and Q'S—Key to Handwriting Analysis,* New York: Key Publishing Co., 1959

MILTON, M., *Handwriting Analysis,* New York: Tower Books, 1970

MYER, O., *The Language of Handwriting*, New York: Stephen Daye Press, 1951

NEVO, BERNARD, Ph.D., *Scientific Aspects of Graphology*, Springfield, ILL: Charles C. Thomas, 1986.

NEZOS, RENNA, *Graphology, the Interpretation of Handwriting*, London, England: Rider & Co. Century Hutchinson Ltd., 1986.

OLYANOVA, N., *Handwriting Tells*, New York: Sterling, 1973

OVERSTREET, B., *Understanding Fear*, New York: Harper, 1951

PELTON, R., *What Your Handwriting Reveals*, New York: Hawthorne Books, 1969

PESKIN, D., *The Art of Job Hunting*, Cleveland, Ohio: World Publishing, 1967

ROMAN, K., *Handwriting, The Key to Personality*, New York: Pantheon, 1952

SASSI, PAULA C.G., WHITING, ELDENE C.G., *Vocational Evaluation*, San Diego, CA, 1985.

SEMLER-DELMAR, BETTY, *Schematic Graphology*, Northbrook, IL: Delmar Graphological Systems, 1987.

SINGER, E., *A Manual of Graphology*, London, England: Duckworth & Co. Ltd., 1969

TAYLOR, R. Preferences of Industrial Managers for Information Sources in Making Promotion Decisions, *Journal of Applied Psychology*, April 1975

THEWLIS, M.; SWEZY, I., *Handwriting and the Emotions*, New York: American Graphological Society, 1954

WESTERGAARD, MARJORIE, *International Directory of Handwriting Analysts*. Various editions.

WHITING, E., Handwriting Secrets, Column, San Diego, CA: North Shores Sentinel, 1964-1972

List of Occupations Appearing in This Book

Index

187

193

194